Taxation Transcripts

Deciphering Enterprise Records for Shareholder Clarity

Ethan Navarro

Table of Contents

1 Chapter 1: Foundations of Tax Record Analysis 5
1.1 Understanding Financial Statements 8
1.2 Key Tax Forms Overview 12

2 Chapter 2: Inventory Valuation Techniques . . . 15
2.1 FIFO vs. LIFO Impacts 18
2.2 Weighted Average Method 21
2.3 Specific Identification 25

3 Chapter 3: Depreciation and Amortization 29
3.1 Straight-Line Depreciation 33
3.2 Accelerated Depreciation Methods 36

4 Chapter 4: Revenue Recognition Principles . . . 41
4.1 Accrual Accounting Insights 44
4.2 Cash Basis Considerations 47
4.3 Sales Return Impact 50

5 Chapter 5: Expense Tracking and Deductions . . 55
5.1 Ordinary and Necessary Expenses 58
5.2 Capital Expenditures vs. Expenses 61
5.3 Deductibility Limitations 64
5.4 Travel and Entertainment Rules 67

5.5 Home Office Deduction 70

6 Chapter 6: Liabilities and Equity Analysis 75

6.1 Understanding Debt Obligations 78

6.2 Shareholder Equity Components 81

6.3 Retained Earnings Analysis 84

7 Chapter 7: Advanced Tax Planning Strategies . . 87

7.1 Tax Credits and Incentives 89

7.2 Minimizing Tax Liabilities 92

1 Chapter 1: Foundations of Tax Record Analysis

Let's dive right into the heart of understanding tax record analysis. The journey begins with grasping the fundamental language of business: financial statements. These aren't just dry documents filled with numbers; they're the narrative of a company's financial health, performance, and future prospects. To truly decipher tax records, you need to become fluent in reading these statements.

Financial statements paint a complete picture. They include the income statement, the balance sheet, and the statement of cash flows. Each statement serves a distinct purpose, but they are intrinsically linked. The income statement, often called the profit and loss (P&L) statement, reveals a company's financial performance over a specific period. It details revenues, expenses, and ultimately, the net income or loss. Understanding how revenue is generated and how expenses are managed is critical for tax analysis. A careful examination of the income statement can reveal potential tax planning opportunities or areas of concern. For instance, unusually high deductions in a particular period might warrant further investigation.

Next is the balance sheet. This provides a snapshot of a company's assets, liabilities, and equity at a specific point in time. It adheres to the fundamental accounting equation: Assets = Liabilities + Equity. Assets represent what the company owns, liabilities represent what the company owes to others, and equity represents the owners' stake in the company. When analyzing tax records, the balance sheet offers valuable insights into a company's financial structure and its ability to meet its obligations. For instance, a high debt-to-equity ratio could indicate a higher risk of financial distress and potentially impact tax planning strategies related to debt financing. Furthermore, the classification of assets as current or non-current can influence depreciation schedules and related tax deductions.

The statement of cash flows is equally crucial. It tracks the movement of cash both into and out of the company during a specific period, categorized into operating, investing, and financing activities. This statement is essential for understanding a company's liquidity and its ability to generate cash from its core operations. Unlike the income statement, which uses accrual accounting (recognizing revenue and expenses when they are earned or incurred, regardless of cash flow), the statement of cash flows focuses solely on actual cash transactions. Analyzing the statement of cash flows can reveal discrepancies between reported earnings and actual cash generation, which may signal potential issues with revenue recognition or expense management that could have tax implications. A strong cash flow from operations is a positive sign, indicating that the company is generating sufficient cash to cover its expenses, invest in its growth, and pay its debts.

Moving beyond the basics of financial statements, we must consider the key tax forms. These are the official documents that companies use to report their income, deductions, and tax liabilities to the relevant tax authorities. Understanding the purpose and structure of these forms is essential for accurate tax record analysis. Some of the most common and important tax forms include Form 1120 for corporate income tax, Form 1065 for partnership income, and various forms for reporting payroll taxes, sales taxes, and excise taxes. Form 1120, for example, requires companies to report their total revenues, deductions, and taxable income, as well as calculate their tax liability based on the applicable tax rates. The form also includes schedules for reporting specific types of income and deductions, such as depreciation expense, charitable contributions, and research and development credits.

Understanding the nuances of key tax forms allows stakeholders to scrutinize the numbers. Take depreciation schedules, often found as attachments to Form 1120. Comparing these schedules across different years can reveal changes in a company's capital investment strategy and its use of different depreciation methods. Moreover, inconsistencies between the depreciation expense reported on the income statement and the depreciation expense claimed on the tax form might indicate errors or aggressive tax planning strategies. Similarly, examining the schedules related to deductions, such as those for research and development expenses or charitable contributions, can provide insights into a company's investment in innovation and its philanthropic activities, as well as its compliance with relevant tax regulations.

Diving deeper into these forms will prove valuable. By familiarizing yourself with the specific line items, instructions, and schedules, you can identify potential areas of interest or concern. Remember, tax forms are designed to provide a standardized format for reporting financial information to the tax authorities, but they also offer a wealth of data that can be used to analyze a company's financial performance, tax planning strategies, and compliance with tax laws. Pay close attention to any footnotes or disclosures that accompany the tax forms, as these can often provide additional context and clarification regarding specific items or transactions. In short, the tax forms are critical to understand.

To be effective in tax record analysis, you need to develop a critical eye. Don't simply accept the numbers at face value. Instead, question the assumptions, investigate the methodologies, and look for potential red flags. Are the revenue recognition policies consistent with industry standards? Are the expense deductions supported by adequate documentation? Are the tax planning strategies aggressive but defensible, or are they potentially abusive? These are the types of questions you should be asking as you analyze tax records. Finally, keep in mind that tax laws and regulations are constantly evolving. Stay up-to-date on the latest changes and how they might impact a company's tax position. Consult with tax professionals and utilize available resources to ensure that your analysis is accurate and informed. In doing so, you will be well-equipped to decipher enterprise records for shareholder clarity and contribute to informed decision-making.

1.1 Understanding Financial Statements

Financial statements serve as the cornerstone of understanding a company's financial health and, consequently, its tax obligations. For shareholders, deciphering these records is paramount to making informed decisions. These documents are more than just numbers; they are a narrative of the company's performance, position, and cash flows, all of which have direct tax implications. The primary financial statements that demand your attention are the income statement, the balance sheet, and the statement of cash flows. Learning to navigate them effectively will unlock valuable insights into a company's tax strategies and potential liabilities.

Let's start with the income statement, often referred to as the profit and loss (P&L) statement. This statement summarizes a company's revenues, costs, and expenses over a specific period, ultimately revealing its net income or net loss. Revenue is the lifeblood of any business, but how it's recognized significantly impacts the tax liability. For example, understanding the difference between revenue recognized today versus over time can influence when taxes are due. Below the revenue line, you'll find the cost of goods sold (COGS), which represents the direct costs associated with producing or acquiring the goods or services sold. Monitoring COGS trends is vital; unexpected increases can signal inventory management issues or supplier price hikes, which could also have tax implications related to inventory valuation methods discussed later in the book. Operating expenses, such as salaries, rent, and marketing costs, are subtracted from gross profit (revenue minus COGS) to arrive at operating income. This figure represents the company's profitability from its core business operations. Interest expense, another line item to scrutinize, is the cost of borrowing money. High-interest expense can indicate excessive debt, potentially leading to financial distress and affecting the company's ability to invest in growth opportunities. This metric is important because interest expense is typically tax-deductible. The final and arguably most critical line on the income statement is net income. This figure represents the company's profit after all expenses, including taxes, have been deducted. Net income is the ultimate measure of profitability and a key driver of shareholder value. However, remember that net income is a financial reporting metric, and taxable income, which determines the actual taxes paid, may differ due to various tax regulations and accounting method choices. Moving on to the balance sheet, which presents a snapshot of a company's assets, liabilities, and equity at a specific point in time. It follows the fundamental accounting equation: Assets = Liabilities + Equity. Assets are what a company owns, liabilities are what it owes, and equity represents the owners' stake in the company. Current assets, such as cash, accounts receivable, and inventory, are expected to be converted into cash or used up within one year. Cash, of course, is the most liquid asset and directly impacts the company's ability to meet its short-term obligations. Accounts receivable represents money owed to the company by its customers. Monitoring accounts receivable is crucial because delays in collection can lead to cash flow problems. Inventory, as discussed earlier, is a significant asset with substantial tax implications. Non-current assets, such as property, plant, and equipment (PP&E), are long-term investments that are used to generate revenue. PP&E is subject to depreciation, which is a tax-deductible expense, as described in a later chapter. Liabilities represent a company's obligations to others. Current liabilities, such as accounts payable and short-term debt, are due within one year. Accounts payable represents money owed to suppliers, whereas short-term debt includes loans and other obligations due in the near term. Non-current liabilities, such as long-term debt, are due beyond one year. High levels of debt can increase a company's financial risk and limit its flexibility. Equity represents the owners' stake in the company and includes items such as common stock, preferred stock, and retained earnings. Retained earnings represent the accumulated profits that have not been distributed to shareholders as dividends. A healthy balance sheet indicates that a company is financially stable and has the resources to meet its obligations and invest in future growth.

The statement of cash flows, often considered the most insightful of the three statements, reveals the movement of cash both into and out of a company during a specific period. This statement is crucial because it shows how a company generates and uses cash, which is essential for its survival. The statement of cash flows is divided into three sections: cash flow from operating activities, cash flow from investing activities, and cash flow from financing activities. Cash flow from operating activities reflects the cash generated from the company's core business operations. This is typically the most important section of the statement of cash flows, as it indicates the company's ability to generate cash from its primary activities. A positive cash flow from operations suggests that the company is generating enough cash to cover its operating expenses and reinvest in the business. Cash flow from investing activities includes cash flows related to the purchase and sale of long-term assets, such as PP&E and investments. A negative cash flow from investing activities typically indicates that the company is investing in its future growth. Cash flow from financing activities includes cash flows related to debt, equity, and dividends. For example, issuing new debt or equity increases cash flow, while repaying debt or paying dividends decreases cash flow. Analyzing the statement of cash flows can reveal a company's ability to meet its short-term obligations, fund its investments, and return cash to shareholders. It can also highlight potential cash flow problems, such as excessive borrowing or insufficient cash generation from operations.

Analyzing financial statements involves comparing them over time and against industry benchmarks. Horizontal analysis involves comparing financial statement items across different periods to identify trends and patterns. For example, you might compare revenue growth, expense increases, and changes in debt levels over the past several years. Vertical analysis involves expressing each item in a financial statement as a percentage of a base amount. For example, on the income statement, each item might be expressed as a percentage of revenue. Ratio analysis involves calculating various financial ratios to assess a company's profitability, liquidity, solvency, and efficiency. Profitability ratios, such as net profit margin, measure how much profit a company generates from its revenue. Liquidity ratios, such as the current ratio, measure a company's ability to meet its short-term obligations. Solvency ratios, such as the debt-to-equity ratio, measure a company's ability to meet its long-term obligations. Efficiency ratios, such as inventory turnover, measure how efficiently a company manages its assets. By carefully analyzing financial statements, shareholders can gain valuable insights into a company's financial health, tax strategies, and potential liabilities.

1.2 Key Tax Forms Overview

Let's navigate the labyrinth of tax forms, a task crucial for any shareholder seeking transparency in enterprise records. While voluminous and seemingly arcane, these forms are, in essence, standardized reports reflecting a company's financial narrative to tax authorities. Understanding their purpose, structure, and content is vital for deciphering a company's financial health and tax compliance. One must realize that it's not about becoming a tax expert overnight, but about gaining enough familiarity to ask the right questions and interpret the information presented.

The cornerstone of corporate tax reporting in many jurisdictions is the corporate income tax return. In the United States, for instance, this is the Form 1120. This form serves as the primary vehicle for companies to calculate and report their taxable income to the government. It outlines a company's total revenues, deductions, and ultimately, its tax liability. What often goes unnoticed is that the detailed schedules attached to Form 1120 are where the true story lies. Schedules detailing cost of goods sold, depreciation, executive compensation, and related-party transactions can offer invaluable insights into a company's operational efficiency and potential tax risks.

Form 1099 is a series of information returns employed to report payments made to individuals or entities who are not employees. Several variations exist, each tailored to specific types of payments. Form 1099-MISC reports payments for services rendered, rents, royalties, and other income. Another critical variant is Form 1099-DIV, used to report dividends and distributions to shareholders. These forms, while seemingly simple, are essential for verifying the accuracy of reported expenses and income. Discrepancies between amounts reported on 1099s and a company's internal records could signal potential underreporting of income or overstated expenses, requiring further investigation. Scrutinizing these forms can reveal valuable insights into a company's dealings with vendors, contractors, and shareholders, and help assess whether these transactions are conducted at arm's length.

Form W-2 is the wage and tax statement that employers must provide to employees, reporting their annual wages and the amount of taxes withheld. Examining W-2 forms, particularly the aggregate amounts reported, can provide insights into a company's compensation structure and its compliance with employment tax regulations. High levels of executive compensation, relative to industry benchmarks, may warrant further scrutiny to ensure they are justifiable and not designed to evade taxes. Discrepancies between total wages reported and the number of employees can also raise red flags, potentially indicating unreported workers or misclassification of employees as independent contractors. Such practices can expose the company to significant penalties and reputational damage.

Then we get to Schedule K-1, a form utilized by pass-through entities such as partnerships, S corporations, and limited liability companies (LLCs) to report each owner's share of the entity's income, deductions, and credits. For shareholders of these types of entities, Schedule K-1 is the key to understanding their individual tax obligations arising from their investment. Analyzing Schedule K-1 can be complex, as it contains numerous line items detailing various types of income and deductions. Shareholders must understand how these items affect their individual tax returns and be vigilant in ensuring that the information reported on Schedule K-1 is consistent with the entity's overall financial performance. Discrepancies or unusual items on Schedule K-1 may warrant further inquiry to ensure accuracy and compliance.

Another important form is the Form 990, which is used by tax-exempt organizations to report their financial activities to the IRS. Although these organizations are not subject to income tax, Form 990 provides valuable insights into their operations, governance, and

financial health. For shareholders of companies that engage in charitable giving or have relationships with tax-exempt organizations, reviewing Form 990 can provide transparency into these activities. Analyzing Form 990 can help assess whether the company's charitable contributions are aligned with its values and whether its relationships with tax-exempt organizations are conducted ethically and transparently. Unusual transactions or excessive compensation paid to executives of the tax-exempt organization may raise concerns.
Now, let's talk about international tax forms. If a company operates internationally, it will likely be required to file additional tax forms to report its foreign income, taxes paid, and compliance with international tax treaties. These forms can be complex and require specialized knowledge to interpret. Form 5471, for example, is used to report information about U.S. persons who are officers, directors, or shareholders of certain foreign corporations. Similarly, Form 8865 is used to report information about U.S. partners in foreign partnerships. Analyzing these forms can help assess a company's international tax exposure and compliance with transfer pricing regulations. Transfer pricing refers to the prices charged between related parties in different countries, and companies must ensure that these prices are arm's length to avoid shifting profits to lower-tax jurisdictions.
A lot of these forms require specific knowledge, to obtain a clear view of the company's current situation. In order to be sure about that, one must not try to do all by himself, it is better to speak with professionals. Navigating this landscape requires diligence and a willingness to seek professional advice when needed. Remember, knowledge is power, and understanding these key tax forms empowers you to make informed decisions and hold management accountable for their tax practices. Remember, the goal is not to become a tax expert but to gain a basic understanding of these forms and their significance, enabling you to ask informed questions and interpret the information presented in a meaningful way.

2 Chapter 2: Inventory Valuation Techniques

Inventory valuation, at its core, is about assigning a monetary value to the goods a company holds for sale. This seemingly simple task has a significant impact on a company's financial statements and, crucially, its tax obligations. Different methods exist, each with its own set of assumptions and consequences. Selecting the right method, or understanding the method a company has chosen, is vital for deciphering enterprise records and ensuring shareholder clarity. The goal of this chapter is to dissect these techniques, offering a clear understanding of their impact on a company's financial health and tax liabilities.

FIFO, or First-In, First-Out, operates under the assumption that the first units of inventory purchased are the first ones sold. In a period of rising prices (inflation), FIFO tends to result in a lower cost of goods sold (COGS) because the older, cheaper inventory is being expensed. This, in turn, leads to a higher net income and, consequently, potentially higher tax liabilities. For example, imagine a retail store that sells widgets. If they bought widgets in January for $10 each and again in March for $12 each, and they sell some widgets in April, FIFO would assume the $10 widgets were sold first. The remaining inventory would be valued at the higher $12 price, reflecting current market value on the balance sheet. The result can be a

tax disadvantage as it increases the taxable profit of the company.
Now, consider LIFO, or Last-In, First-Out. As the name suggests, LIFO assumes that the last units purchased are the first ones sold. This method is permitted under U.S. GAAP but is prohibited under IFRS. In inflationary environments, LIFO can result in a higher COGS, as the more expensive, recently purchased inventory is expensed. This leads to a lower net income and potentially lower tax liabilities. Using the same widget example, LIFO would assume the $12 widgets were sold first. In this scenario, the cost of goods sold would be higher, lowering taxable income. However, it's worth emphasizing that the remaining inventory would be undervalued on the balance sheet, as it would reflect the older, cheaper prices. The disadvantage of LIFO is that the inventory left has older values than the current market values.
The Weighted Average method offers a different approach. It calculates a weighted average cost for all inventory items available for sale during a period. This average cost is then used to determine both the COGS and the value of ending inventory. The formula for the weighted average cost is: (Total Cost of Goods Available for Sale) / (Total Units Available for Sale). For instance, if a company has 100 widgets at $10 each and then buys another 100 widgets at $12 each, the weighted average cost would be (($10 \emph{ 100) + ($12 } 100)) / 200 = $11. This $11 average cost is then applied to each unit sold and each unit remaining in inventory.
Furthermore, the Specific Identification method is used when a company can clearly identify each specific item in its inventory and track its actual cost. This method is best suited for companies dealing with unique, high-value items, such as custom jewelry, real estate, or specialized equipment. For example, an art gallery would use specific identification because each painting has a unique cost. Similarly, a car dealership would use it to track the cost of each individual vehicle. The advantage of specific identification is its accuracy, as it

precisely matches costs with revenues. However, it can be complex to implement and maintain, especially for businesses with a large volume of inventory. Also, this method can also be subject to manipulation if the business can decide which item it has sold.

Understanding the impact of each inventory valuation technique is crucial for several reasons. First, it directly affects a company's financial statements, particularly the income statement and balance sheet. A higher net income due to FIFO, for example, might attract investors, but it also means a higher tax bill. Conversely, a lower net income under LIFO could reduce tax liabilities but potentially deter some investors. Second, the choice of inventory valuation method can influence key financial ratios, such as the gross profit margin and inventory turnover ratio, which are used by analysts to assess a company's profitability and efficiency. Thirdly, the consistency principle in accounting requires companies to use the same inventory valuation method from one period to the next, unless there's a justifiable reason for a change. Changes in accounting methods can have a significant impact on financial reporting and require proper disclosure. However, the impact isn't limited to financial statements; tax implications are equally important. As mentioned earlier, the choice between FIFO and LIFO can have a significant effect on a company's tax liability, especially in inflationary or deflationary environments. A company must consider its tax planning strategy when selecting an inventory valuation method. For instance, a company anticipating rising prices might choose LIFO to defer taxes, while a company expecting stable or falling prices might opt for FIFO. It's also important to consider the regulatory environment, as tax laws regarding inventory valuation can vary across jurisdictions. It's necessary to consult with tax professionals to ensure compliance and optimize tax outcomes.

Ultimately, the optimal inventory valuation technique depends on a variety of factors, including the nature of the business, industry practices, tax regulations, and the company's overall financial strategy. While FIFO can provide a more accurate representation of current inventory value and can increase profits in times of rising prices, LIFO can offer tax advantages. The weighted average method is simpler to implement and provides a more stable cost basis, while specific identification is ideal for businesses dealing with unique, high-value items. The best approach is to carefully evaluate each method in light of the specific circumstances and objectives of the company, to make sure that the choice is right for you.

2.1 FIFO vs. LIFO Impacts

Inventory valuation significantly influences reported earnings and tax liabilities. The choice between First-In, First-Out (FIFO) and Last-In, First-Out (LIFO) can dramatically alter a company's financial picture, particularly during periods of fluctuating prices. For beginners, understanding these two methods is crucial for interpreting financial statements and assessing a company's tax strategy.
FIFO assumes that the first units purchased are the first units sold. In simpler terms, the oldest inventory is assumed to be sold first. This method often aligns with the actual physical flow of inventory, especially for perishable goods or items with expiration dates. However, its impact on financial reporting can be substantial, particularly during inflationary periods. Let's say a company buys widgets at $10 each in January and then buys the same widgets at $12 each in March. If they sell some widgets in April, FIFO assumes the $10 widgets were sold first. This results in a lower cost of goods sold (COGS) and a higher net income. This higher net income translates to a higher tax liability. Conversely, during deflationary periods, FIFO can lead to a higher COGS, lower net income, and therefore, lower taxes. This simplicity and intuitive nature are benefits, but the tax implications require careful consideration. It is very impor-

tant for companies to understand that the choice between these two methods depends on their industry and specific circumstances.

LIFO, on the other hand, assumes that the last units purchased are the first units sold. In the same scenario as before, LIFO would assume the $12 widgets were sold first. During inflationary periods, this results in a higher COGS and a lower net income, which translates to a lower tax liability. This is often the primary appeal of LIFO for companies operating in industries experiencing rising costs. However, LIFO can result in a lower reported profit, which some investors may view negatively, because the income would be lower. In a deflationary environment, the opposite is true – LIFO can lead to a lower COGS, higher net income, and higher taxes. Further complicating matters, the Internal Revenue Service (IRS) has specific rules regarding LIFO. If a company uses LIFO for tax purposes, it must also use LIFO for financial reporting purposes. This is known as the LIFO conformity rule. These complex rules require careful adherence.

The impact of FIFO and LIFO extends beyond just the income statement. These methods also affect the balance sheet. Under FIFO, the ending inventory is valued at the most recent purchase prices. This can be seen as a more accurate representation of the current market value of inventory. However, under LIFO, the ending inventory is valued at the oldest purchase prices. During inflationary times, this can result in an understated inventory value on the balance sheet. Investors need to be aware of these differences when comparing companies that use different inventory valuation methods. For example, a company using LIFO might appear to have lower assets compared to a similar company using FIFO, even if their actual physical inventory is the same. So, the method significantly affects both the income statement and the balance sheet, which will impact shareholders' decisions.

The decision of which method to use, FIFO or LIFO, is not a simple one. Many factors must be considered, including the nature of the inventory, the industry, the expected direction of prices, and the tax implications. For instance, companies dealing with rapidly changing technology or fashion trends might prefer FIFO to ensure their inventory is valued closer to current market prices. Meanwhile, companies in industries with stable or rising prices might opt for LIFO to minimize their tax liabilities. However, the potential for lower reported profits under LIFO needs to be carefully weighed against the tax benefits. To better understand the advantages and disadvantages, companies must carefully consider them.

Furthermore, the availability of LIFO is limited in some countries. International Financial Reporting Standards (IFRS), used in many countries outside the United States, do not permit the use of LIFO. This means that companies operating globally may need to use different inventory valuation methods for different reporting purposes. This adds another layer of complexity to the inventory accounting process. If a company does not operate in the United States, it might not be allowed to use LIFO.

In practice, many companies use a combination of inventory valuation methods. For example, a company might use FIFO for some types of inventory and LIFO for others. They might also use the weighted-average method or specific identification for certain items. The key is to choose the method that best reflects the company's specific circumstances and provides the most accurate picture of its financial performance. This understanding of FIFO and LIFO is essential for shareholders and stakeholders because it allows them to make sound decisions based on accurate data.

Another important factor to consider is the potential for LIFO liquidation. This occurs when a company sells more inventory than it purchases during a period. When this happens, older, lower-cost inventory layers are liquidated, resulting in a higher profit and a higher tax liability. LIFO liquidation can distort a company's financial results and make it difficult to compare its performance over time. Therefore, companies using LIFO need to carefully manage their inventory levels to avoid unintended LIFO liquidations. This distortion should always be avoided in any case scenario, and is also a problem for FIFO users, so a combination of techniques is a good solution.

Choosing between FIFO and LIFO isn't just about accounting rules. It's about understanding your business, predicting market trends, and strategically managing your tax obligations. If you're new to analyzing financial statements, pay close attention to the inventory valuation method a company uses. It can tell you a lot about their operations and their approach to financial management. By understanding the implications of FIFO and LIFO, you'll be better equipped to make informed investment decisions and assess a company's true financial health. A great understanding is necessary to properly invest in the stock market.

To make it easier to analyze the differences, consider the following points: FIFO generally results in a higher net income during inflationary periods, while LIFO results in a lower net income. FIFO leads to a higher ending inventory value on the balance sheet, while LIFO can lead to an understated inventory value. LIFO is not permitted under IFRS, while FIFO is widely accepted. The choice between FIFO and LIFO depends on the specific circumstances of the company and its industry. In conclusion, these two methods heavily influence the company's assets, net income, and therefore the business's profitability.

2.2 Weighted Average Method

When deciphering enterprise records, grasping the weighted average method for inventory valuation is essential. It's a cornerstone of financial accounting that impacts both a company's reported profits and its tax obligations, offering a smoothed representation of inventory costs compared to other methods. It allows for a more reliable picture of the financial situation.

The core idea behind the weighted average method is deceptively simple: you calculate the average cost of all available inventory during a period and use that average cost to determine the value of both the cost of goods sold (COGS) and the ending inventory. This contrasts with methods like FIFO (First-In, First-Out) or LIFO (Last-In, First-Out), which assume that specific units are sold first. To start, you must know the total cost of goods available for sale, which includes the beginning inventory value plus the cost of all purchases made during the accounting period. Then, you divide this total cost by the total number of units available for sale, including beginning inventory and purchases. This calculation gives you the weighted average cost per unit. Next, multiply the number of units sold by this average cost to determine the cost of goods sold. Finally, multiply the number of units remaining in ending inventory by the average cost to determine the value of ending inventory. While seeming simple, it gets more complex in practice, so always use assistance.

Let's illustrate with a scenario. Imagine a company, "Acme Gadgets," which starts January with 100 gadgets in inventory, each costing \$10. Throughout January, Acme Gadgets makes two additional purchases: 200 gadgets at \$12 each and 150 gadgets at \$11 each. By the end of January, Acme Gadgets sells 300 gadgets. Calculating the weighted average cost involves several steps. First, determine the total cost of goods available for sale: (100 gadgets \emph{ \$10) + (200 gadgets } \$12) + (150 gadgets \emph{ \$11) = \$1000 + \$2400 + \$1650 = \$5050. Next, determine the total number of units available for sale: 100 + 200 + 150 = 450 gadgets. Now, calculate the weighted average cost per gadget: \$5050 / 450 gadgets = \$11.22 (rounded to the nearest cent). To find the cost of goods sold, multiply the number of gadgets sold by the weighted average cost: 300 gadgets } \$11.22

= $3366. Finally, calculate the value of ending inventory: (450 total gadgets \item 300 gadgets sold) \emph{ $11.22 = 150 gadgets } $11.22 = $1683. This provides a much clearer understanding of what the company situation looks like.

The weighted average method offers several advantages. Simplicity is a major draw, making it easier to implement and understand compared to FIFO or LIFO, especially for businesses with a large volume of similar inventory items. Cost averaging provides a smoother representation of inventory costs, reducing the impact of price fluctuations on a company's financial statements. In volatile markets, this can be particularly beneficial, preventing significant swings in reported profits due to temporary price spikes or dips. However, it is not a perfect solution.

While the weighted average method is simple, it has drawbacks. It can mask the true cost of goods sold if there are significant fluctuations in purchase prices, leading to a less accurate reflection of the actual cost flow. Unlike specific identification, which tracks the cost of each individual item, the weighted average method assumes a uniform cost, which might not be realistic for businesses dealing with heterogeneous inventory. Further, from a tax perspective, the weighted average method may not offer the same tax benefits as LIFO in inflationary environments. LIFO can often reduce taxable income during periods of rising prices, potentially leading to lower tax liabilities. Therefore, always consider these pros and cons.

Choosing the right inventory valuation method is not merely an accounting decision, it's a strategic one with far-reaching implications for a company's financial reporting and tax obligations. Shareholders must understand how these choices impact reported earnings, inventory values, and tax liabilities to effectively assess a company's financial health and performance. The weighted average method provides a reasonable and straightforward approach to inventory valuation, offering a balance between simplicity and accuracy. However, it is crucial to weigh its benefits against its limitations and consider whether it aligns with the company's specific inventory management practices and tax planning objectives. The choice of method should be based on a thorough understanding of the business, its industry, and its financial goals. It is best to always analyze the financial situation before deciding.

Now, let's consider how the weighted average method interacts with shareholder clarity. Transparency in financial reporting is paramount for building trust with shareholders. The weighted average method, with its relatively simple calculations and ease of understanding, can contribute to this transparency. When a company uses the weighted average method, it should clearly disclose this fact in its financial statements, along with a detailed explanation of how the method is applied. This disclosure allows shareholders to understand how inventory costs are determined and how they affect the company's reported profits. However, just disclosing the method is not enough. Shareholders also need to understand the potential impact of this method on the company's financial performance, especially in comparison to other methods. For example, if a company switches from FIFO to weighted average, shareholders should be informed of the reasons for the change and the expected impact on reported earnings and tax liabilities. This provides a better understanding of all the available options.

Finally, from a shareholder's perspective, understanding the weighted average method can empower you to ask informed questions and make better investment decisions. By understanding how inventory costs are determined, shareholders can better assess the company's profitability, efficiency, and financial health. When analyzing a company's financial statements, pay attention to the disclosures related to inventory valuation methods. Compare the company's inventory turnover ratio to its competitors, considering the potential impact of different valuation methods. Analyze the company's gross profit margin and operating income, taking into account how the weighted average method might affect these metrics. Ask management questions about their inventory management practices and how they choose to value inventory. All of these factors are important.

2.3 Specific Identification

Specific Identification, while potentially meticulous, offers unparalleled accuracy in inventory valuation. Unlike FIFO, LIFO, or weighted average, this method directly links the cost of each specific item to its sale, providing a crystal-clear picture of your cost of goods sold and taxable income. This chapter will guide you through the process of implementation, explore the advantages and disadvantages, and highlight situations where it shines.

The core principle is simple: maintain a precise record of the purchase cost for each individual item in your inventory. When that item is sold, you directly assign its specific cost to the cost of goods sold. Consider a car dealership. Each vehicle has a unique Vehicle Identification Number (VIN) and a specific purchase price. When a particular car is sold, the dealership knows exactly what it cost to acquire that specific car, allowing for precise cost allocation. This contrasts sharply with, say, a grocery store using FIFO for milk cartons, where the cost of the oldest cartons is always assumed to be the cost of goods sold, regardless of which specific carton was purchased.

Implementing this system requires meticulous record-keeping from the outset. Upon receiving inventory, each item must be uniquely identified, often through tagging or serial numbers, and its purchase cost diligently recorded. Spreadsheets, specialized inventory management software, or even a dedicated database can be employed. The key is to establish a robust tracking system that follows each item from acquisition to sale. For smaller businesses with limited inventory or high-value, easily distinguishable items, a simple spreadsheet might suffice. Larger operations with diverse inventory likely require sophisticated software capable of handling complex tracking needs. This initial setup can be time-consuming, but the long-term benefits in terms of accuracy and control can be substantial.

There are distinct advantages to employing specific identification. First and foremost, it offers unparalleled accuracy in determining the cost of goods sold and, consequently, taxable income. This accuracy translates to improved financial reporting and a reduced risk of errors in tax filings. Second, it eliminates the potential for manipulating profits through inventory valuation, a risk inherent in FIFO and LIFO. Specific identification provides a true representation of actual costs, enhancing transparency and credibility with stakeholders. Third, it is particularly advantageous for businesses dealing with high-value, low-volume items. Think art galleries, antique shops, or custom jewelry businesses. In these cases, the individual cost of each item is significant, and using an averaging method would distort the true profitability of each sale.

But be aware, specific identification also presents several disadvantages. The most significant hurdle is the increased administrative burden. Maintaining detailed records for each individual item requires significant time and effort. This can be especially challenging for businesses with a high volume of inventory or complex supply chains. This increased complexity can translate to higher administrative costs, potentially offsetting the benefits of increased accuracy. Furthermore, the method can be impractical for businesses dealing with homogenous goods, where individual items are indistinguishable. Consider a grain elevator or a gasoline distributor; tracking the specific cost of each grain of wheat or gallon of gasoline would be virtually impossible. Finally, specific identification may not be permitted under certain accounting standards or tax regulations in some jurisdictions. Always consult with a qualified accountant or tax advisor to ensure compliance.

Let us explore situations where specific identification shines. As mentioned previously, businesses dealing in high-value, low-volume items are prime candidates. Art galleries, antique dealers, jewelers, and car dealerships all benefit from the accuracy and transparency this method provides. Furthermore, businesses that manufacture custom-made products often find specific identification useful. They can directly track the costs of materials and labor associated with each individual order, allowing for precise pricing and profit margin analysis. Businesses subject to stringent regulatory requirements may also find specific identification appealing. The enhanced accuracy and traceability can help demonstrate compliance and reduce the risk of penalties.

Think of a small, family-owned jewelry store specializing in custom-designed pieces. Each piece is unique, with varying costs of gold, gemstones, and labor. Using specific identification, the jeweler can meticulously track the cost of each component and the time spent crafting each piece. When a custom ring is sold, the jeweler can precisely determine the cost of goods sold, leading to a more accurate calculation of profit and taxable income. This level of detail is simply not achievable with other inventory valuation methods.

On the other hand, consider a large supermarket chain. They sell thousands of units of identical products daily. Trying to track the specific cost of each can of soup or bag of potatoes would be a logistical nightmare. In this case, FIFO or weighted average would be far more practical and efficient. The key is to assess the nature of your inventory, the volume of sales, and the administrative resources available before deciding whether specific identification is the right choice.

Successfully implementing specific identification requires careful planning and execution. Start by clearly defining the scope of your inventory and establishing a unique identification system for each item. This could involve assigning serial numbers, using barcode scanners, or implementing RFID tags. Invest in appropriate inventory management software that can track individual items and their associated costs. Train your staff on the proper procedures for receiving, storing, and selling inventory, emphasizing the importance of accurate record-keeping. Regularly reconcile your inventory records with physical inventory counts to identify and resolve any discrepancies. Finally, consult with a qualified accountant or tax advisor to ensure compliance with all applicable accounting standards and tax regulations.

In closing, while specific identification demands meticulous attention to detail, it rewards businesses with unparalleled accuracy and transparency in inventory valuation. By carefully weighing the advantages and disadvantages, and by implementing a robust tracking system, you can determine whether this method is the right fit for your specific needs. Remember, understanding the nuances of inventory valuation is crucial for making informed financial decisions and optimizing your company's tax position.

3 Chapter 3: Depreciation and Amortization

Imagine a newly purchased delivery van. It's not just about the upfront cost; you need to factor in how that van loses value over time. That loss of value, that's depreciation. It represents the wearing out, the obsolescence, and the gradual decline in the van's ability to perform its intended purpose. Amortization is similar, but it applies to intangible assets, like a patent, a software license, or even a franchise agreement. These assets don't have a physical presence, but they provide value to the business over a specific period. Understanding how these concepts work is crucial for accurately interpreting a company's financial health and tax obligations. The proper handling of depreciation and amortization is vital in ensuring a transparent and fair view of a company's profits and tax liabilities.

Straight-line depreciation is perhaps the most straightforward method. Think of it as spreading the cost of an asset evenly over its useful life. Let's say that delivery van cost \$30,000, and you estimate it will be useful for five years. Also, we will calculate the salvage value. Salvage value is what you think the van will be worth at the end of those five years – maybe \$5,000. The depreciable base would be \$25,000 (\$30,000 \item \$5,000). With straight-line depreciation, you would deduct \$5,000 (\$25,000 / 5 years) in depreciation expense each year for five years. This method is simple, predictable, and easy to understand, making it a common choice for many businesses, especially small ones. While it may not perfectly reflect the actual decline in value of an asset, its simplicity makes it a practical and consistent approach. Many times it can give a first glimpse of how the company handles finances. The clarity of this approach can be beneficial for the shareholders to understand how their company's assets are losing value over time.

Accelerated depreciation methods, on the other hand, recognize that an asset may lose more of its value in the early years of its life. One popular method is the double-declining balance method. With this method, you calculate the straight-line depreciation rate (in our van example, that was 20% per year). Then, you double that rate (to 40%). In the first year, you would apply that 40% rate to the full cost of the asset ($30,000 x 40% = $12,000). In the second year, you apply the 40% rate to the remaining book value of the asset (the original cost minus accumulated depreciation). So, in year two, the calculation would be (($30,000 \item $12,000) x 40% = $7,200). Notice that depreciation expense is higher in the early years and lower in the later years. There are also Sum-of-the-Years' Digits method which has a decreasing amount to depreciate yearly and this requires the addition of the digits of the asset's useful life to determine the denominator (a 5 year old asset would sum $5 + 4 + 3 + 2 + 1 = 15$). Each year the depreciation expense is determined by calculating the remaining years over the sum of the years, and then multiplying that fraction by the depreciable base. The first year it would be $5/15$ of the depreciable base. These accelerated methods can be beneficial for tax purposes, as they allow for larger deductions in the early years of an asset's life. This can reduce taxable income and improve cash flow in the short term.

When deciding which depreciation method to use, several factors should be considered. The nature of the asset, its expected usage pattern, and the tax implications are all important. For assets that are expected to decline in value rapidly in the early years, an accelerated method may be more appropriate. For assets that are used evenly over their lives, straight-line depreciation may be a better fit. Tax laws also play a significant role, as certain methods may be more advantageous from a tax perspective. For example, some jurisdictions allow for bonus depreciation or Section 179 expensing, which allows businesses to deduct the full cost of an asset in the year it is placed in service. The company needs to make an informed decision that is aligned with the best interest of its stakeholders.

Amortization, while similar to depreciation, applies to intangible assets. Consider a company that acquires a patent for a new technology. The cost of that patent can be amortized over its useful life, typically its legal life or its estimated economic life, whichever is shorter. The most common method for amortization is the straight-line method, where the cost of the intangible asset is spread evenly over its useful life. For example, if a patent costs $100,000 and has a useful life of 10 years, the amortization expense would be $10,000 per year. Unlike depreciation, intangible assets typically do not have a salvage value, so the entire cost is amortized. Understanding amortization is essential for assessing the value of a company's intangible assets and their impact on its financial statements. It provides a more complete picture of a company's overall financial health. This is an important element for shareholders who seek understanding of how the company is doing.

Depreciation and amortization directly impact a company's financial statements. Depreciation expense reduces net income on the income statement, which in turn affects retained earnings on the balance sheet. Accumulated depreciation, which is the total depreciation expense recognized on an asset over its life, is a contra-asset account that reduces the book value of the asset on the balance sheet. Similarly, amortization expense reduces net income and increases accumulated amortization. These accounting entries affect key financial ratios, such as return on assets and debt-to-equity, which are used by investors and analysts to evaluate a company's performance and financial position. Therefore, a thorough understanding of depreciation and amortization is crucial for interpreting financial statements accurately.

From a tax perspective, depreciation and amortization are deductible expenses that reduce taxable income. The choice of depreciation method can have a significant impact on a company's tax liability, particularly in the early years of an asset's life. Accelerated depreciation methods result in larger deductions in the early years, which can reduce taxable income and lower tax payments. However, over the long term, the total amount of depreciation that can be claimed is the same regardless of the method used (as long as the asset is held for all its useful life). It's important for businesses to understand the tax implications of different depreciation methods and to choose the method that is most advantageous for their specific circumstances. Tax planning strategies often involve optimizing depreciation deductions to minimize tax liabilities.

Shareholders should pay close attention to how a company accounts for depreciation and amortization. Inconsistent or aggressive depreciation practices can distort a company's financial performance and mislead investors. For instance, if a company significantly extends the useful lives of its assets, it can artificially reduce depreciation expense and boost net income. This can make the company appear more profitable than it actually is. Similarly, aggressive amortization practices can inflate the value of intangible assets on the balance sheet. Investors should carefully review a company's accounting policies and disclosures related to depreciation and amortization to ensure that they are reasonable and consistent. A healthy dose of skepticism is always warranted when evaluating financial statements.

Ultimately, depreciation and amortization are vital concepts for understanding how companies account for the declining value of their assets. They affect both financial reporting and tax obligations, and they have a significant impact on a company's financial statements. By understanding these concepts, shareholders can gain a deeper insight into a company's financial health and make more informed investment decisions. The methods used for depreciation and amortization, as well as the assumptions underlying those methods, can provide valuable clues about a company's management practices and its overall financial strategy. Therefore, this chapter offers a compass for steering through the often opaque waters of corporate accounting.

3.1 Straight-Line Depreciation

Depreciation, in its essence, is the allocation of an asset's cost over its useful life. The straight-line method stands as the simplest and most widely understood approach to this process. It's a cornerstone of accounting, providing a predictable and consistent way to recognize the decline in value of an asset due to wear and tear, obsolescence, or simply the passage of time. This method assumes that an asset depreciates evenly over its lifespan, making it particularly attractive for its ease of calculation and application.

Understanding straight-line depreciation is not merely an academic exercise; it's a fundamental skill for anyone seeking to analyze a company's financial health and tax position. As a shareholder, grasping how a company depreciates its assets can provide valuable insights into its capital investment strategy, its profitability, and its tax liabilities. It allows you to interpret financial statements with a more critical eye, discerning whether a company's reported earnings accurately reflect the economic reality of its operations.

The formula for straight-line depreciation is remarkably straightforward: (Asset Cost \item Salvage Value) / Useful Life. Let's break down each component. The asset cost is the original price paid for the asset, including any costs directly related to getting it ready for its intended use, such as installation or transportation. The salvage value is the estimated value of the asset at the end of its useful life; this is the amount the company expects to receive from selling or disposing of the asset after it is no longer used in operations. The useful life is the estimated number of years or units of output that the asset is expected to be used by the company. It's important to remember that the useful life is an estimate, and it can be influenced by factors such as technological advancements, industry practices, and the company's maintenance policies. Imagine a company purchases a delivery truck for $50,000. They estimate that the truck will have a salvage value of $5,000 after five years of use. Using the straight-line method, the annual depreciation expense would be ($50,000 - $5,000) / 5 = $9,000. This $9,000 would be recorded as an expense on the income statement each year, reducing the company's taxable income.

The simplicity of the straight-line method comes with both advantages and disadvantages. One of the main advantages is its ease of use and understanding. It requires minimal calculations and is easily explained to stakeholders, making financial statements more transparent. Moreover, the constant depreciation expense over the asset's life provides a stable and predictable impact on the company's earnings, which can be beneficial for financial planning and forecasting. However, the straight-line method may not accurately reflect the actual depreciation pattern of all assets. Some assets, such as machinery or equipment, may experience greater depreciation in their early years due to higher usage or technological obsolescence. In such cases, accelerated depreciation methods may provide a more realistic portrayal of the asset's decline in value. Furthermore, the straight-line method does not consider the time value of money, meaning that it treats depreciation expense in the first year the same as depreciation expense in the last year, even though the former has a greater impact on the company's present value.

While the straight-line method simplifies depreciation, its impact on financial statements is significant. The annual depreciation expense reduces net income, which in turn affects earnings per share (EPS), a key metric for investors. A higher depreciation expense leads to lower net income and EPS, which could potentially dampen investor sentiment. However, it's important to remember that depreciation is a non-cash expense, meaning that it does not involve an actual outflow of cash. Therefore, while depreciation reduces net income, it also reduces taxable income, resulting in lower tax payments. This tax shield can have a positive impact on the company's cash flow, which is crucial for its long-term sustainability. Depreciation also affects the balance sheet. Each year, the accumulated depreciation, which is the total depreciation expense recognized on an asset to date, is recorded as a contra-asset account, reducing the asset's book value. This book value, also known as the net book value, represents the asset's carrying value on the balance sheet.

Different industries may favor different depreciation methods based on the nature of their assets and their operational needs. Companies in industries with rapidly changing technology, such as software or electronics, may opt for accelerated depreciation methods to reflect the faster obsolescence of their assets. Conversely, companies in industries with long-lived assets, such as real estate or infrastructure, may find the straight-line method more suitable. Understanding the industry context is crucial for interpreting a company's depreciation policies. If a company is using the straight-line method when its industry peers are using accelerated methods, it may indicate that the company is trying to artificially inflate its earnings. On the other hand, if a company is using accelerated methods when its industry peers are using the straight-line method, it may indicate that the company is trying to reduce its tax liabilities.

As a shareholder, it's essential to scrutinize the company's disclosures about its depreciation policies in the financial statement footnotes.

These disclosures provide details about the depreciation methods used, the estimated useful lives of the assets, and the amount of depreciation expense recognized each year. They also provide information about any changes in depreciation methods or estimates, which can have a significant impact on the company's financial results. By carefully reviewing these disclosures, you can gain a deeper understanding of the company's capital investment strategy and its efforts to manage its earnings and tax liabilities. Don't hesitate to ask questions if you find anything unclear or inconsistent. Engaging with the company's management or investor relations team can provide valuable insights into their depreciation policies and their rationale for choosing specific methods and estimates.
Ultimately, straight-line depreciation, despite its simplicity, offers a vital window into a company's financial practices and its understanding of its own assets. By understanding its mechanics, its advantages and disadvantages, and its impact on financial statements, shareholders can make more informed decisions about their investments. It's not just about numbers; it's about understanding the story behind the numbers and the choices that shape a company's financial destiny.

3.2 Accelerated Depreciation Methods

Accelerated depreciation methods offer a faster write-off of an asset's cost compared to the straight-line approach, recognizing that assets often contribute more to revenue in their early years. Understanding these methods is essential for shareholders to assess a company's reported earnings and tax liabilities accurately. While straight-line depreciation spreads the cost evenly over the asset's useful life, accelerated methods front-load the depreciation expense, leading to higher deductions in the initial years and lower deductions later on. This can have significant implications for a company's financial statements and tax obligations, as a greater depreciation expense reduces taxable income and, consequently, the tax liability in the short term. One prominent accelerated depreciation method is the double-declining balance (DDB) method. To calculate depreciation under DDB, one first determines the straight-line depreciation rate, typically 1 divided by the asset's useful life in years. This rate is then doubled, and the resulting percentage is applied to the asset's book value (cost less accumulated depreciation) each year. It's crucial to remember that the DDB method does not consider the salvage value initially. However, depreciation should cease when the asset's book value equals its salvage value, ensuring the asset is not depreciated below this level. The DDB method can provide substantial tax benefits in the early years of an asset's life, allowing a company to defer taxes and improve its cash flow position. However, it is important to be aware that in the later years, the depreciation expense will be lower than under the straight-line method, potentially leading to higher taxable income.

Another common accelerated method is the sum-of-the-years' digits (SYD) method. Under SYD, depreciation is calculated by multiplying the asset's depreciable base (cost less salvage value) by a fraction. The numerator of this fraction represents the remaining years of the asset's useful life, while the denominator is the sum of the digits of all the years of the asset's useful life. For instance, if an asset has a 5-year useful life, the denominator would be 1 + 2 + 3 + 4 + 5 = 15. In the first year, the numerator would be 5, resulting in a depreciation expense of (5/15) * (cost \item salvage value). In the second year, the numerator would be 4, and so on. The SYD method, while not as aggressively accelerated as DDB, still provides higher depreciation expense in the early years of the asset's life compared to the straight-line method. The selection of this method depends on several factors, including the company's tax strategy and expectations about the asset's productivity over its lifespan.

A critical aspect of using accelerated depreciation methods lies in their potential impact on a company's financial ratios. Higher depreciation expense in the early years reduces reported earnings, which can lead to lower profitability ratios such as net profit margin and return on assets. However, it is important to remember that these ratios are affected by accounting choices, and accelerated depreciation does not necessarily reflect a company's underlying economic performance. Shareholders should carefully analyze the company's depreciation policy and its impact on financial ratios to gain a comprehensive understanding of its financial health. Moreover, comparing a company's depreciation methods with those of its peers can provide insights into its accounting practices and financial reporting strategies.

Beyond the standard accelerated methods, tax laws often provide for bonus depreciation or Section 179 expensing, which allow companies to deduct a significant portion or even the entire cost of an asset in the year of purchase. These provisions are designed to incentivize investment in new equipment and stimulate economic growth. While they can provide substantial tax savings, they also require careful planning and consideration of the long-term tax implications. Shareholders should be aware of the availability of these provisions and their potential impact on a company's tax liability and cash flow. Furthermore, understanding the rules and limitations associated with bonus depreciation and Section 179 expensing is crucial for assessing the quality of a company's earnings and its tax planning strategies.

The choice of depreciation method can also affect a company's deferred tax liabilities or assets. Accelerated depreciation methods create a temporary difference between the book value of an asset for financial reporting purposes and its tax basis. This difference gives rise to a deferred tax liability, which represents the future tax obligation that will arise when the asset is fully depreciated for tax purposes but still has a remaining book value for financial reporting purposes. On the other hand, if a company uses straight-line depreciation for tax purposes and an accelerated method for financial reporting, it will create a deferred tax asset. Understanding deferred tax liabilities and assets is essential for shareholders to assess a company's long-term tax obligations and its overall financial health. Analyzing the changes in deferred tax accounts can provide valuable insights into a company's tax planning strategies and its ability to manage its tax liabilities effectively.

In conclusion, accelerated depreciation methods offer a valuable tool for companies to manage their tax liabilities and improve their cash flow, particularly in the early years of an asset's life. However, shareholders must carefully analyze the company's depreciation policy, its impact on financial ratios, and its long-term tax implications to gain a comprehensive understanding of its financial health and its ability to generate sustainable returns. While higher depreciation expense in the early years can reduce reported earnings, it can also lead to lower tax liabilities and improved cash flow, which can benefit shareholders in the long run. Therefore, a thorough understanding of accelerated depreciation methods is essential for making informed investment decisions and assessing a company's financial performance accurately. It is vital to check the business strategies to see what is more reliable for tax reduction plans in the long run.

4 Chapter 4: Revenue Recognition Principles

Revenue recognition is the cornerstone of financial reporting. It dictates when and how a company acknowledges revenue, directly impacting reported profitability and, subsequently, tax obligations. Shareholders must grasp these principles to accurately interpret financial statements and assess a company's true financial health. Ignoring revenue recognition practices can lead to a distorted view of a company's performance, potentially masking underlying issues or inflating perceived success. The seemingly simple question of when to recognize revenue has immense implications for understanding a company's tax picture.

Accrual accounting, the prevalent method for most large businesses, recognizes revenue when it is earned, regardless of when cash is received. This means that if a company delivers goods or services in one period but doesn't get paid until the next, the revenue is recognized in the period of delivery. The core principle revolves around the transfer of goods or services and the expectation of payment. Consider a software company that sells a subscription. While they might receive the entire payment upfront, under accrual accounting, they recognize revenue ratably over the subscription period. This provides a more accurate depiction of the company's financial performance over time, avoiding a one-time revenue spike followed by periods of seemingly low income. The matching principle, a key component of accrual accounting, dictates that expenses should be recognized in the same period as the revenues they help generate. Therefore, costs associated with delivering a service, like employee salaries or server maintenance for the software company, are also recognized over the subscription period, aligning revenue and expenses to paint a clearer financial picture. Understanding this relationship provides deeper insight.

Cash basis accounting, primarily used by smaller businesses or individuals, recognizes revenue only when cash is received. This method is simpler but less precise in reflecting economic reality, particularly for businesses with significant accounts receivable or long sales cycles. If a small consultancy performs services in December but gets paid in January, they would recognize the revenue in January under the cash basis. This method can lead to distortions in reported income, especially if revenue or expenses fluctuate significantly between periods. The Internal Revenue Service (IRS) has specific guidelines on who can use the cash basis, generally limiting it to smaller businesses with average annual gross receipts below a certain threshold. The choice between accrual and cash basis impacts not only the timing of revenue recognition but also the complexity of record-keeping. While the cash basis offers simplicity, it might not accurately represent a company's financial performance, potentially misleading shareholders. A company showing high profit under cash basis might actually be near bankrupcy.

Sales returns present a unique challenge to revenue recognition. When a company sells goods with a right of return, they must estimate the amount of sales returns they expect and reduce revenue accordingly. This estimation is critical for ensuring accurate financial reporting. For instance, a clothing retailer must account for the potential returns of items purchased during the holiday season. They would estimate the return rate based on historical data and industry benchmarks, reducing the initially recognized revenue to reflect this expectation. Furthermore, they need to establish a reserve for estimated returns, essentially setting aside funds to cover potential refunds. This reserve impacts both the balance sheet and the income statement, reflecting the company's commitment to honoring returns and the corresponding reduction in net income. If the actual returns significantly differ from the estimated amount, adjustments must be made in subsequent periods, highlighting the importance of accurate forecasting. Failure to properly account for sales returns can lead to overstated revenue, potentially misleading shareholders about the company's financial performance and triggering scrutiny from regulators. The amount of sales returns must be a good balance.

Understanding these principles allows shareholders to scrutinize a company's revenue recognition policies and practices. Red flags might include aggressive revenue recognition practices, such as recognizing revenue prematurely or failing to adequately account for sales returns. By carefully examining a company's financial statements and footnotes, shareholders can assess the reasonableness of their revenue recognition policies and identify potential accounting issues. Remember that a company's financial health is not just about the numbers; it's about how those numbers are generated and reported. Being able to decipher the nuances of revenue recognition is crucial to truly understand a company's profitability and the sustainability of its success. For example, if a company consistently recognizes revenue at the earliest possible moment, even with significant uncertainty about collectability, it might be artificially inflating its reported earnings. This could be a sign of financial distress or an attempt to mislead investors. So, analyze the records diligently.

Moreover, consider the industry in which the company operates. Different industries have different revenue recognition standards and practices. For example, a construction company recognizes revenue differently than a software company. A construction company

might use the percentage-of-completion method, recognizing revenue as work progresses on a project. Shareholders need to understand the specific revenue recognition methods used within a particular industry to accurately compare companies and assess their financial performance. It becomes even more important with more and more complex markets, where the company's financial picture is more important than ever.
Ultimately, revenue recognition is not just an accounting concept; it's a lens through which shareholders can view a company's financial performance and integrity. By understanding these principles, shareholders can ask insightful questions, challenge management's assumptions, and make informed investment decisions. The better the understanding, the best and most accurate investment decisions will be.

4.1 Accrual Accounting Insights

Accrual accounting stands as a cornerstone of modern financial reporting, offering a significantly more comprehensive view of a company's financial performance than the cash basis method. It operates on the principle of recognizing revenue when earned and expenses when incurred, regardless of when the cash actually changes hands. This timing difference creates a crucial layer of complexity and nuance in the analysis of enterprise records, particularly when deciphering them for shareholder clarity. For instance, consider a software company that provides a subscription service. Under accrual accounting, the revenue from a one-year subscription is not recognized entirely upfront when the customer pays. Instead, it is recognized ratably over the twelve-month period as the service is delivered. This provides a more accurate reflection of the company's ongoing performance and prevents a single large payment from distorting the financial picture in a particular quarter.

Understanding the impact of accrual accounting on key financial statements is paramount. The income statement, under accrual accounting, presents a more accurate picture of profitability by matching revenues with the expenses incurred to generate those revenues. This matching principle is essential for assessing the true efficiency and profitability of a business. For instance, if a company incurs significant marketing expenses in one period to generate sales in a subsequent period, the accrual method ensures that these expenses are recognized in the same period as the related revenue, providing a clearer understanding of the return on investment. The balance sheet, also influenced by accrual accounting, reflects assets and liabilities that are not necessarily represented by immediate cash transactions. Accounts receivable, for example, represent revenue that has been earned but not yet collected in cash, while accounts payable represent expenses that have been incurred but not yet paid. These accruals provide a more comprehensive view of a company's financial position and its obligations.
Delving deeper, the nuances of accrual accounting require a careful examination of specific accounts and their potential impact on tax liabilities. Deferred revenue, a common accrual account, represents payments received for goods or services that have not yet been delivered. While the cash has been received, the revenue is not recognized for accounting purposes until the obligation is fulfilled. This can create a timing difference between when the cash is received and when the revenue is taxable. Similarly, accrued expenses, such as salaries or interest, represent expenses that have been incurred but not yet paid. These accruals are typically deductible for tax purposes in the period they are incurred, even if the cash payment is made in a later period. The treatment of these accruals can significantly impact a company's taxable income and its overall tax liability.
For shareholders, grasping the implications of accrual accounting is essential for making informed investment decisions. By understand-

ing how revenue and expenses are recognized under this method, shareholders can gain a more accurate assessment of a company's true financial performance and its underlying economic health. A company that consistently reports strong profits under accrual accounting is generally more stable and sustainable than one that relies solely on cash-based accounting, which can be easily manipulated. However, it's crucial to scrutinize the quality of earnings reported under accrual accounting. Aggressive or overly optimistic revenue recognition practices, such as recognizing revenue prematurely or underestimating potential sales returns, can artificially inflate reported profits and create a misleading picture of the company's performance. Furthermore, analyzing the changes in accrual accounts over time can provide valuable insights into a company's financial health. A significant increase in accounts receivable, for example, may indicate that the company is struggling to collect payments from its customers, potentially signaling financial difficulties. Conversely, a decrease in accounts payable may indicate that the company is paying its suppliers more quickly, which could be a sign of strong cash flow management. By carefully monitoring these trends, shareholders can identify potential red flags and make more informed decisions about their investments. This involves comparing a company's accrual ratios with industry benchmarks to identify any unusual patterns or deviations that may warrant further investigation.

Moreover, understanding the link between accrual accounting and tax regulations is crucial for assessing a company's tax compliance and its ability to manage its tax liabilities effectively. While accrual accounting is generally required for financial reporting purposes, certain exceptions may apply for tax purposes, particularly for smaller businesses. However, for larger corporations, accrual accounting is typically required for both financial reporting and tax purposes. This alignment ensures consistency and transparency in the reporting of financial information. However, there can still be differences in the timing of revenue and expense recognition between accounting and tax rules, leading to deferred tax assets and liabilities. These deferred taxes represent the future tax consequences of temporary differences between the book and tax bases of assets and liabilities. Analyzing these deferred taxes can provide insights into a company's tax planning strategies and its potential future tax obligations.

In conclusion, accrual accounting provides a more accurate and comprehensive view of a company's financial performance than cash-based accounting. By understanding the principles of accrual accounting and its impact on key financial statements, shareholders can gain a deeper understanding of a company's true financial health and its ability to generate sustainable profits. Careful scrutiny of accrual accounts and their trends over time, along with an understanding of the link between accrual accounting and tax regulations, is essential for making informed investment decisions and assessing a company's long-term value. Shareholders must remain vigilant in their analysis of accrual accounting data, recognizing that while it offers valuable insights, it is not without its limitations. Always consider the overall economic context and industry-specific factors when interpreting financial information derived from accrual accounting methods.

4.2 Cash Basis Considerations

Cash basis accounting, while simpler than accrual accounting, presents unique considerations when analyzing a company's tax records and its implications for shareholders. Unlike accrual accounting, where revenue is recognized when earned and expenses are recognized when incurred, the cash basis method recognizes revenue when cash is received and expenses when cash is paid out. This fundamental difference can lead to a vastly different picture of a company's financial health, particularly regarding tax liabilities. My aim here is to guide you through understanding those considerations.

The most immediate impact of using the cash basis is on the timing of taxable income. A business might have performed services or delivered goods, but if payment hasn't been received by year-end, the revenue isn't taxable until the cash comes in, in the subsequent year. Similarly, if a company purchases supplies in December but doesn't pay for them until January, the expense deduction is delayed until the following year. This can create situations where a company appears more or less profitable in a given year than it actually is, affecting the apparent tax liability. This is where a deeper dive into the context is needed. You need to look at the consistency of application from year to year to understand if there are manipulations taking place or if the impact is an anomaly.

When examining financial records of cash-basis businesses, you must always consider the potential for delayed or accelerated recognition of income and expenses. For example, a business owner anticipating a higher tax rate in the following year might delay payments to vendors to push the deduction into the higher-tax year. Conversely, they might accelerate invoicing and collection efforts to recognize more income in a year with a lower tax rate, or offset a year of high expenses. Such practices, while legal, can obscure the true economic performance of the company. For instance, an unusually high amount of accounts payable at year-end might signal a conscious effort to defer expenses and inflate current-year earnings.

The eligibility to use the cash basis is often restricted to smaller businesses, primarily due to its simplicity. Generally, corporations (other than S corporations) and partnerships with a C corporation partner, as well as tax shelters, are generally barred from using the cash method if their average annual gross receipts exceed $25 million for the three prior tax years (as of 2018, and adjusted for inflation in subsequent years). If a company's gross receipts fluctuate around this threshold, it might be required to switch between the cash and accrual methods, creating complex transitional adjustments. These adjustments can significantly impact reported income and tax liabilities in the year of the switch and subsequent years. This makes it very important to review the accounting method the business uses over time.

The simplicity of the cash basis can also mask underlying financial issues. Because revenue and expenses are recorded only when cash changes hands, there's a potential for a distorted view of the company's true profitability. A company might appear highly profitable based on cash flow, but it could also be accumulating significant debt or failing to reinvest in its operations. Shareholders need to be aware of these limitations and look beyond the immediate cash position to assess the company's long-term sustainability. The point is to review the expenses and understand where resources have been directed in the company.

Proper scrutiny of related party transactions is particularly important in cash-basis businesses. Because of the flexibility in timing income and expenses, there's a greater opportunity to shift profits and losses between related entities to minimize overall tax liability. For example, a business owner might delay paying themselves a salary to reduce their personal income tax, or they might accelerate payments to a related company to reduce its taxable income. Such transactions require careful examination to ensure they are conducted at arm's length and for legitimate business purposes.

Beyond the income statement, the cash basis significantly impacts the balance sheet. Under the cash method, there are no accounts receivable or accounts payable, as these are only recognized under accrual accounting. This simplifies the balance sheet, but it also means that shareholders must rely on other sources of information to assess the company's short-term liquidity. For instance, they might need to review bank statements, sales records, and vendor invoices to gain a complete picture of the company's working capital position.

Moreover, the cash method can affect inventory management. Un-

der the accrual method, inventory is capitalized as an asset and expensed as cost of goods sold when the inventory is sold. Under the cash method, inventory purchases are often expensed immediately, regardless of whether the goods have been sold. This can result in significant fluctuations in reported income, particularly for businesses with substantial inventory holdings. It also creates an incentive to manage inventory levels to minimize tax liability.
Finally, consider the implications for long-term planning. The cash method provides limited insight into a company's future financial performance. Because it focuses on current cash flows, it doesn't account for future revenue streams or expenses that are already committed. This can make it difficult to assess the company's long-term prospects and to make informed investment decisions. Shareholders should seek additional information, such as sales forecasts, backlog reports, and capital expenditure budgets, to gain a more complete understanding of the company's strategic direction. Cash accounting is a helpful method when used correctly, but it doesn't tell the whole story and you, as a shareholder, need to understand the limitations of that perspective.

4.3 Sales Return Impact

Sales returns represent a significant challenge in revenue recognition, particularly because they introduce uncertainty about the actual amount of revenue a company will ultimately realize. When a company sells goods or services, it anticipates receiving payment for them. However, customers may return products for various reasons, such as defects, dissatisfaction, or simply changing their minds. These returns directly impact the top line and, consequently, the tax liabilities. Understanding how to properly account for and report sales returns is crucial for maintaining accurate financial records and ensuring compliance with tax regulations. Failing to properly account for these returns can distort a company's financial picture, leading to miscalculations of taxable income and potential penalties from tax authorities.

The accrual accounting method, commonly used by larger businesses, mandates that revenue is recognized when earned, not necessarily when cash is received. This principle becomes complex when sales returns are involved. While a sale might initially seem complete, the possibility of a return means the revenue isn't entirely certain. To address this uncertainty, companies estimate the amount of future returns and reduce their reported revenue accordingly. This estimation process is crucial because it directly affects the income statement and the balance sheet. On the income statement, estimated sales returns decrease reported revenue, leading to a lower gross profit. On the balance sheet, a corresponding entry is made to establish a sales returns allowance, a contra-asset account that reduces the value of accounts receivable. The accuracy of this estimation is paramount; an underestimated allowance could result in overstated revenues and profits, while an overestimated allowance could artificially depress earnings.

The tax implications of sales returns are intrinsically linked to how they are handled in financial accounting. Tax regulations generally follow accounting principles regarding revenue recognition, meaning that if a sales return reduces reported revenue for financial reporting purposes, it will also affect taxable income. Let's consider a scenario where a company anticipates $10,000 in sales returns. This $10,000 reduction in revenue would directly lower the company's gross income, leading to a decreased tax liability. However, it is important to note that tax authorities may scrutinize the reasonableness of the sales returns estimate. If the tax authorities deem the estimate to be excessive or unsubstantiated, they may disallow the deduction, resulting in a higher tax bill. Therefore, maintaining detailed records of sales returns, along with the rationale behind the estimation methodology, is essential for supporting the company's tax position.

Documenting the sales returns process is a cornerstone of sound financial and tax management. Companies must maintain meticulous records of all sales transactions, including those involving returns. This documentation should include the date of sale, the item sold, the reason for the return, and the date of the return. Furthermore, the company should document the methodology used to estimate future sales returns. This documentation should outline the factors considered, such as historical return rates, seasonal trends, and any specific events that may impact return patterns. For example, a product recall or a change in warranty policy could significantly alter the expected rate of returns. The documentation should be clear, concise, and readily accessible for both internal audits and external reviews by tax authorities. A well-documented sales returns process not only facilitates accurate financial reporting but also provides a solid defense against potential tax disputes.

From a shareholder's perspective, understanding a company's sales returns policy and its impact on financial statements is essential for making informed investment decisions. High sales return rates can indicate potential problems with product quality, customer satisfaction, or marketing strategies. A significant increase in sales returns could signal a decline in the company's competitive position or a shift in consumer preferences. Therefore, shareholders should carefully examine the company's financial statements, paying close attention to the sales returns allowance and the related disclosures. Analyzing the trends in sales returns over time can provide valuable insights into the company's performance and its ability to generate sustainable revenue. Moreover, shareholders should consider comparing the company's sales returns rate to industry averages to assess whether the company's performance is in line with its peers. A high sales return rate relative to the industry could warrant further investigation.

Sales return policies are not just accounting procedures; they are intertwined with customer service strategies and warranty provisions. A generous return policy can attract customers and build brand loyalty, but it can also lead to higher return rates and increased costs. On the other hand, a restrictive return policy may deter some customers and damage the company's reputation. Finding the right balance between customer satisfaction and cost management is crucial. The company's warranty policy also plays a significant role. If a product is covered by a warranty, customers are more likely to return it for repairs or replacements, impacting the sales returns process. Companies should carefully consider the costs and benefits of different return and warranty policies and design them in a way that maximizes customer value while minimizing financial risks.

The materiality of sales returns also dictates the level of scrutiny required. If sales returns are a relatively small percentage of total revenue, they may not warrant extensive analysis. However, if sales returns are material, meaning they could influence the decisions of investors or creditors, they require careful attention. In such cases, companies may need to engage external auditors to review their sales returns process and ensure the accuracy of their financial reporting. Material sales returns may also trigger additional disclosures in the company's financial statements, providing investors with more detailed information about the nature and extent of the returns. By understanding the materiality of sales returns, companies can tailor their accounting and reporting practices to meet the needs of their stakeholders.

The continuous monitoring and adjustment of sales returns estimates are crucial for maintaining accuracy. Sales patterns and consumer behavior can shift, requiring businesses to adapt their forecasting methods. This involves regularly reviewing historical data, analyzing market trends, and considering any new factors that could impact sales returns. For example, if a company launches a new product line, it should closely monitor the return rates for that product and adjust its estimates accordingly. Similarly, if the company enters a new geographic market, it should take into account the local consumer preferences and return practices. By continuously monitoring and adjusting their sales returns estimates, companies can improve the accuracy of their financial reporting and minimize the risk of tax errors.

Considering specific examples of how companies handle sales returns is vital for understanding the practical application of these principles. A large retailer, for instance, may use sophisticated data analytics to predict sales returns based on factors such as product category, customer demographics, and purchase history. A software company might offer a trial period with a money-back guarantee, which requires careful tracking of refund requests. A manufacturing company might face returns due to product defects, necessitating a robust quality control process and a system for processing warranty claims. Each of these examples highlights the unique challenges and considerations associated with sales returns in different industries. By studying these examples, businesses can gain valuable insights into how to effectively manage their sales returns process and ensure accurate financial reporting.

5 Chapter 5: Expense Tracking and Deductions

Expense tracking and deductions form the bedrock of minimizing a company's tax burden, a crucial area directly impacting profitability and shareholder value. Understanding which expenses are deductible, and to what extent, requires careful attention to detail and a thorough understanding of tax regulations. The core principle revolves around the concept of "ordinary and necessary" expenses, the gatekeepers to legitimate deductions. An expense is considered ordinary if it is common and accepted in the particular trade or business. Necessary means that the expense is helpful and appropriate for the business. Note that an expense does not have to be indispensable to be considered necessary. These expenses are directly subtracted from revenue to arrive at taxable income, thus reducing the amount of tax owed. However, proving that an expense meets this criterion is where meticulous record-keeping becomes paramount. Without proper documentation, the IRS may disallow the deduction, leading to increased tax liabilities. For instance, marketing expenses, salaries, and rent are typically considered ordinary and necessary for most businesses, but clear records showing the purpose and amount of each expenditure are vital.

Distinguishing between capital expenditures and expenses is a critical step to ensure accuracy. Capital expenditures are investments in assets that will benefit the business for more than one year, such as buildings, equipment, or land. These expenditures are not immediately deductible. Instead, they are capitalized and depreciated or amortized over their useful lives. Depreciation allows a business to deduct a portion of the asset's cost each year, reflecting its gradual decline in value. Expenses, on the other hand, are costs incurred for the day-to-day operations of the business and are generally deductible in the year they are incurred. Misclassifying a capital expenditure as an expense can lead to an overstatement of deductions in the current year and an understatement of taxable income. Conversely, failing to capitalize an asset can result in a missed opportunity to claim depreciation deductions over time. An example includes the purchase of a delivery van, a capital expenditure subject to depreciation over several years, in contrast to fuel costs, a current expense deductible in the year incurred.

Even if an expense is considered ordinary and necessary, it may still be subject to deductibility limitations. Tax laws often impose restrictions on the amount that can be deducted for certain types of expenses. One common limitation applies to business meals, where only 50% of the cost is generally deductible. This rule is in place to prevent abuse and ensure that deductions are reasonable. Another common area of limitation involves charitable contributions. Corporations can generally deduct charitable contributions up to 10% of their taxable income. Contributions exceeding this limit can be carried forward and deducted in future years, subject to similar limitations. Understanding these limitations is crucial to avoid overstating deductions and facing potential penalties from the IRS. For example, excessive spending on client entertainment, even if intended to generate business, may not be fully deductible due to these limitations. Navigating the rules surrounding travel and entertainment expenses can be particularly complex. To be deductible, travel expenses must be primarily for business purposes. This means that the majority of the trip must be devoted to business activities, not personal leisure. Documentation is critical here, including detailed itineraries, receipts for transportation and lodging, and records of business meetings. Entertainment expenses, as mentioned earlier, are generally subject to the 50% deductibility limitation. Furthermore, they must be directly related to or associated with the active conduct of the business. Simply taking a client out for a casual meal may not qualify if there is no substantive business discussion. Keep records of who was in attendance, the purpose of the entertainment, and how it benefited the business. An example includes traveling to a conference to network with potential clients and attend industry-specific seminars, contrasting with a weekend getaway with minimal business interactions.

The home office deduction allows eligible taxpayers to deduct expenses related to the business use of their home. To qualify, the home office must be used exclusively and regularly as the principal place of business, or as a place to meet with clients or customers. The deduction is limited to the gross income derived from the business activity conducted in the home. This means that you cannot deduct more than you earn from your business. Eligible expenses include mortgage interest, rent, utilities, insurance, and depreciation. Calculating the deduction involves determining the percentage of the home used for business purposes, typically based on square footage. This percentage is then applied to the total eligible expenses to determine the deductible amount. For instance, using a spare bedroom solely for business operations, calculating the percentage of the home it occupies, and then applying that percentage to expenses like mortgage interest and utilities, allows for an appropriate deduction. Maintaining detailed records of all home-related expenses is necessary to substantiate the deduction.

5.1 Ordinary and Necessary Expenses

Defining what constitutes an "ordinary and necessary" expense is central to understanding deductible business costs. The Internal Revenue Service (IRS) allows businesses to deduct expenses that are both ordinary and necessary. Ordinary refers to expenses that are common and accepted in your industry. Necessary means the expense is helpful and appropriate for your trade or business. It doesn't have to be indispensable, but it should be conducive to the business's operations. This distinction is crucial because it dictates which costs can be legally subtracted from your gross income, thereby reducing your tax liability. Think of it this way: buying office supplies is ordinary for most businesses, and necessary for daily operations, making it deductible. This principle applies across a wide range of industries, from retail to professional services, but the specifics of what qualifies can vary considerably.

The concept of "ordinary" isn't about being a frequent expense, but rather that it's a typical cost within your industry. If you're a software developer, subscribing to a coding resource platform is an ordinary expense. For a restaurant, purchasing food supplies is ordinary. Even if you only incur certain expenses occasionally, they can still be considered ordinary if they're a standard part of doing business in your sector. The IRS often refers to industry standards and practices to determine whether an expense meets this criterion. Documentation is key here; maintain records that show the expense is commonly accepted within your field. For instance, if you attend an industry conference, keep brochures and agendas to demonstrate its relevance to your business.

On the other hand, the "necessary" component means the expense aids your business. It doesn't need to be absolutely essential for your survival, but it needs to be helpful in developing your business. An expense would not be considered necessary if it's purely personal or lavish. If you hire a consultant to improve your marketing strategy, that's a necessary expense. Buying a company car is necessary if it is used for business activities like client visits or transporting equipment. Remember, the IRS is concerned with expenses that are directly related to your business's revenue-generating activities.

Distinguishing between ordinary and necessary expenses can be complex and requires careful consideration. Some expenses might seem ordinary at first glance but fail the "necessary" test. For instance, extravagant office decorations might be commonplace in some high-end firms, but if they don't directly contribute to business development or productivity, they might be disallowed as deductions. Conversely, some necessary expenses might appear unusual but are indeed ordinary within a specific niche. Consider a specialized manufacturing firm needing to purchase a rare and costly piece of equipment. While not a common expense for all businesses, it is ordinary and necessary for that particular operation.

Documentation plays a vital role in supporting your expense deductions. Keep detailed records, including receipts, invoices, and any supporting documentation that proves the business purpose of the expense. If you are audited, you'll need solid evidence to justify your deductions. It's not enough to simply state that an expense was business-related; you need to provide proof. For example, if you claim a deduction for travel expenses, keep a log of your trips, including the dates, destinations, and business reasons for each trip. Similarly, if you're deducting expenses for client meals, note the names of the clients, the topics discussed, and how the meal contributed to your business relationships.

Certain categories of expenses require extra vigilance. Travel and entertainment expenses, for example, are frequently scrutinized by the IRS. The rules surrounding these deductions can be tricky, and it's easy to make mistakes. Remember that you generally can't deduct expenses that are considered lavish or extravagant. You must also have a clear business purpose for the expense, such as meeting with clients or attending a conference. Home office deductions also fall under close scrutiny. To claim this deduction, you must use a portion of your home exclusively and regularly for business purposes. You can't deduct expenses for a space that's also used for personal activities.

Understanding industry-specific guidelines is also important. What is considered ordinary and necessary can vary significantly depending on the type of business you operate. For example, a construction company might deduct the cost of heavy equipment rentals, while a consulting firm might deduct the cost of professional development courses for its employees. Researching the typical expenses in your field can help you identify what is likely to be considered ordinary and necessary. You can consult with industry associations, tax professionals, or even review IRS publications that address specific industries.

Navigating the complexities of ordinary and necessary expenses can be challenging, but it's an essential aspect of managing your tax liability effectively. By understanding the rules, keeping detailed records, and seeking professional advice when needed, you can ensure that you're claiming all the deductions you're entitled to while staying compliant with tax laws. Failing to properly document and justify your expense deductions can lead to penalties and interest, so it's worth investing the time and effort to get it right. Accurate record-keeping not only helps with tax compliance but also provides valuable insights into your business's financial health, allowing you to make informed decisions about your spending and investments. By prioritizing accurate tracking and a deep understanding of what qualifies as ordinary and necessary, you'll optimize your tax position and create a more financially sound operation.

5.2 Capital Expenditures vs. Expenses

Differentiating between capital expenditures and expenses is a fundamental concept in financial accounting and tax compliance, crucial for accurately reflecting a company's financial performance and determining its tax obligations. Misclassifying these items can significantly distort a company's financial statements, leading to incorrect profitability assessments and potentially triggering tax penalties. The difference lies in the enduring benefit of the expenditure. A capital expenditure (CAPEX) provides a benefit extending beyond the current accounting period, while an expense provides a benefit consumed within the current accounting period.

Capital expenditures are investments in assets that are expected to generate revenue or provide benefits for more than one accounting period. These assets are typically recorded on the balance sheet and depreciated or amortized over their useful lives. Common examples include the purchase of new machinery, buildings, land, or significant improvements to existing assets. The key characteristic of a capital expenditure is that it increases the value of an asset, extends its useful life, or adapts it to a new or different use. For instance, if a company purchases a new printing press, it's a capital expenditure. Or, consider a factory roof that's starting to leak. Repairing a small leak is typically an expense, but replacing the entire roof is a capital expenditure because it extends the life of the building. Think of it this way: will this purchase or improvement offer value to the company over several years? If so, it's likely a capital expenditure.

On the other hand, expenses are costs incurred in the normal course of business to generate revenue within the current accounting period. They are recorded on the income statement and deducted from revenue to arrive at net income. Examples of expenses include salaries, rent, utilities, advertising, and the cost of goods sold. The defining feature of an expense is that its benefit is consumed within the current period. Take, for instance, a small business owner who buys printer paper. That paper is used up quickly, contributing to the day-to-day operation of the business. Or consider the monthly electricity bill, the cost of which is directly related to operating the business during that month. These are clear examples of expenses that are fully deductible in the period they are incurred.

The distinction between capital expenditures and expenses has significant implications for a company's financial statements. Capital expenditures are not immediately expensed but are instead capitalized as assets on the balance sheet. The cost of these assets is then gradually expensed over their useful lives through depreciation or amortization. This process spreads the cost of the asset over the periods it benefits, providing a more accurate picture of the company's profitability in each period. Expenses, however, are immediately deducted from revenue in the period they are incurred, directly impacting the company's net income. For example, a company that incorrectly classifies a large capital expenditure as an expense will significantly understate its net income in the current period, while overstating it in subsequent periods. In simple terms, capitalizing expenditures spreads out the cost over time, while expensing them recognizes the entire cost immediately.

From a tax perspective, the classification of an expenditure as capital or expense has a direct impact on a company's taxable income. Expenses are immediately deductible, reducing taxable income in the current period. Capital expenditures, on the other hand, are not immediately deductible but are instead depreciated or amortized over their useful lives, providing a tax deduction each year. This difference in timing can significantly affect a company's cash flow and overall tax liability. Consider a small business that invests in a new delivery van. Instead of deducting the entire cost of the van in the year of purchase, the business will depreciate the van over several years, deducting a portion of its cost each year. This impacts the

timing of tax deductions, affecting the company's cash flow.
Several factors can complicate the determination of whether an expenditure should be classified as capital or expense. One common area of confusion is repairs and maintenance. Routine repairs that maintain an asset's existing condition are typically treated as expenses, while significant improvements that extend the asset's useful life or increase its value are considered capital expenditures. The key is to assess whether the repair simply restores the asset to its original condition or if it enhances the asset beyond its original state. For example, fixing a broken window in a building is an expense, while replacing all the windows with energy-efficient ones is a capital expenditure. Another area of complexity is the cost of software. The cost of off-the-shelf software is generally treated as an expense, while the cost of developing custom software is typically capitalized and amortized over its useful life.
To ensure accurate classification of expenditures, companies should establish clear accounting policies and procedures. These policies should provide guidance on how to evaluate the nature of an expenditure and determine whether it meets the criteria for capitalization. Companies should also maintain detailed records of all expenditures, including supporting documentation to justify the classification decision. Regular review of these policies and procedures by qualified accounting professionals is essential to ensure compliance with accounting standards and tax regulations. For instance, a company might create a checklist to evaluate each expenditure, considering factors such as the cost, useful life, and impact on the asset's value. Regular training for accounting staff is also crucial.
Ultimately, correctly classifying capital expenditures and expenses is vital for accurate financial reporting and tax compliance. It provides a clear picture of a company's financial performance, helps to allocate the cost of assets over their useful lives, and ensures that tax obligations are properly calculated. Shareholder clarity is enhanced when

companies consistently and accurately apply these principles. By implementing sound accounting policies and seeking professional advice when needed, companies can navigate the complexities of expenditure classification and ensure that their financial statements provide a true and fair view of their financial position. For those entrusted with the stewardship of shareholder value, a meticulous approach to these details is not merely good practice – it is a cornerstone of responsible corporate governance.

5.3 Deductibility Limitations

Understanding the intricacies of deductibility limitations is paramount for any shareholder seeking to decipher enterprise records and assess the true tax implications affecting their investment. Tax laws, while aiming for fairness, often impose restrictions on the amount or type of expenses a business can deduct, impacting net income and ultimately, shareholder value. This isn't about finding loopholes; it's about navigating the rules correctly.

Certain expenses, while legitimately incurred by a business, may face limitations on their deductibility due to specific tax code provisions. A prime example is the limitation on the deductibility of business interest expense. Section 163(j) of the Internal Revenue Code imposes limitations on the amount of business interest that can be deducted in a tax year. The limitation generally applies to businesses with average annual gross receipts exceeding a certain threshold, which is adjusted annually for inflation. The deductible amount is generally limited to the sum of business interest income plus 30% of the adjusted taxable income of the business. Disallowed interest expense can be carried forward indefinitely to future tax years. This provision aims to curb excessive leveraging by companies, but it can significantly impact those relying heavily on debt financing. It's crucial to understand how this limitation affects a company's reported

taxable income and its long-term financial strategy.
Another area ripe with deductibility limitations lies in the realm of meals and entertainment expenses. While businesses can deduct ordinary and necessary expenses, the rules surrounding meals and entertainment are particularly stringent. Generally, only 50% of business meal expenses are deductible, and specific conditions must be met. The meal must not be lavish or extravagant under the circumstances, and the taxpayer or an employee of the taxpayer must be present at the meal. Furthermore, the meal must be directly related to or associated with the active conduct of the taxpayer's trade or business. Entertainment expenses, such as taking clients to sporting events or concerts, are generally not deductible. These rules aim to prevent abuse and ensure that deductions are limited to genuine business-related activities. When analyzing expense records, shareholders must be aware of these limitations and scrutinize the documentation supporting these deductions. Are the meals properly documented, showing the business purpose and attendees? Are entertainment expenses being improperly claimed? These details can significantly affect the accuracy of the reported taxable income.
Moving beyond meals and entertainment, consider the limitations on deducting losses from certain activities, particularly those classified as "passive activities." Passive activities are generally defined as businesses in which the taxpayer does not materially participate. Losses from passive activities can only be deducted to the extent of passive income. If a business has passive losses exceeding passive income, the excess losses are suspended and carried forward to future years. This rule prevents taxpayers from using losses from passive investments to offset income from active businesses. Shareholders should carefully examine the nature of a company's investments and activities to determine if any losses are subject to the passive activity loss rules. This is particularly relevant for real estate activities and investments in partnerships or S corporations. Understanding these limitations

can reveal potential tax liabilities that might not be immediately apparent from a cursory review of the financial statements.

Furthermore, the deductibility of certain payments may be limited under the provisions related to related-party transactions. These rules are designed to prevent businesses from shifting income to related parties in lower tax brackets or artificially inflating expenses. For instance, if a company makes payments to a shareholder or a subsidiary at inflated rates, the deductions may be disallowed or limited. The Internal Revenue Service closely scrutinizes related-party transactions to ensure they are conducted at arm's length, meaning that the terms are comparable to those that would be negotiated between unrelated parties. Shareholders should be wary of transactions between the company and its insiders, particularly if the terms appear to be unusually favorable to the related party. These transactions could indicate potential tax avoidance schemes that could ultimately harm shareholder value.

Another area of consideration is the limitation on the deductibility of charitable contributions. While charitable contributions are generally deductible, there are percentage limitations based on the taxpayer's adjusted gross income. For corporations, the deduction for charitable contributions is generally limited to 10% of taxable income. Contributions exceeding this limit can be carried forward for up to five years. Shareholders should review the company's charitable giving policies to ensure they are in compliance with these limitations. Large or unusual charitable contributions could be a red flag, particularly if they appear to be motivated by tax avoidance rather than genuine philanthropic intent.

The deductibility of expenses related to lobbying and political activities is also subject to limitations. Businesses cannot deduct expenses incurred for lobbying state or federal legislators or for participating in political campaigns. These rules aim to ensure that taxpayers are not subsidizing political activities through tax deductions. Shareholders should examine the company's expense records for any indications of lobbying or political expenditures. These expenses may be disguised as consulting fees or other business expenses, so it's essential to carefully scrutinize the details of these transactions.

Finally, it's critical to remember the consistent application of accounting methods. Switching accounting methods, even if seemingly beneficial for tax purposes, requires careful consideration and often the consent of the IRS. Inconsistencies or unauthorized changes in accounting methods can lead to significant adjustments and potential penalties. A company might choose to switch from LIFO to FIFO, impacting reported income. Shareholders must be vigilant in identifying any accounting method changes and assessing their impact on the company's financial statements and tax liabilities. It is necessary to ensure that the changes are properly justified and disclosed.

By understanding these common deductibility limitations, shareholders can gain a deeper understanding of a company's tax position and identify potential risks or opportunities. Analyzing enterprise records with an awareness of these limitations is crucial for making informed investment decisions and protecting shareholder value.

5.4 Travel and Entertainment Rules

Navigating the world of travel and entertainment (T&E) expenses within a corporate setting can feel like traversing a legal mine field. One wrong step, and you risk running afoul of the Internal Revenue Service (IRS) regulations, potentially leading to penalties and unwanted scrutiny. It's a balancing act, ensuring legitimate business activities are supported while preventing personal expenses from being disguised as business ones. Understanding the nuances of what is deductible, what is not, and how to properly document everything is paramount for both the company and its shareholders. After all, shareholders have a vested interest in ensuring that the company's tax practices are compliant and efficient, as this directly impacts the company's profitability and ultimately their returns.

The cornerstone of deductibility for T&E expenses lies in the concept of being "ordinary and necessary." This means that the expense must be common and accepted in your industry and helpful to the business. Ordinary, in this context, doesn't mean that it's a daily occurrence, but rather that it's a customary and reasonable expense for businesses in your field. Necessary implies that the expense is appropriate and helpful for the business's trade or business. So, taking a client out for dinner to discuss a potential deal could qualify, while a purely social outing, even with a client, might not. This is where meticulous record-keeping becomes crucial. Don't assume anything is deductible, start from the place that is not and prove it is, because the burden of proof lies with the taxpayer.

A key point to grasp is the substantiation requirements. The IRS mandates that you meticulously document T&E expenses, not just with receipts, but with detailed records that answer the "who, what, when, where, and why" of each expenditure. A simple receipt from a restaurant showing the total bill isn't enough. You need to note who you were with, their business affiliation, the specific business discussed, and how the meal directly related to your business. For travel expenses, you'll need to keep records of your itinerary, the dates of travel, the purpose of the trip, and receipts for transportation, lodging, and other incidental expenses. It's not just about proving you spent the money; it's about proving it was for a legitimate business purpose. Without proper substantiation, the IRS can disallow the deduction, leaving the company to shoulder the full cost without any tax benefit. Remember that reconstruction is not enough, you need to be able to prove everything.

Entertainment expenses have a specific set of rules that significantly impact their deductibility. Under current tax law, many entertainment expenses are not deductible, or have very specific exceptions.

This changed significantly a few years ago, so what was once deductible might not be anymore. Generally, entertainment expenses must be directly related to, or associated with, the active conduct of your trade or business. What does this mean? A business discussion must occur directly before, during, or after the entertainment. Furthermore, there need to be the existence of a clear business purpose for incurring the cost. This rules out taking clients to sporting events or concerts merely for goodwill purposes, unless you have a substantial business discussion at or around the event. The IRS has become increasingly strict in scrutinizing entertainment expenses, so it's more important than ever to document everything meticulously and err on the side of caution.

Travel expenses are another area where careful attention to detail is required. While traveling for business, you can generally deduct transportation costs (airfare, train tickets, car rentals), lodging, meals, and incidental expenses. However, if a trip is primarily for personal reasons, even if some business is conducted, you can only deduct the expenses that are directly related to the business portion of the trip. For example, if you extend a business trip to include a vacation, you can deduct the costs of getting to and from your business destination, but not the extra days spent vacationing. Keep detailed records of your itinerary and all associated expenses to substantiate your deductions. Also, remember that lavish or extravagant expenses are not deductible, so choose reasonable accommodations and transportation options. The goal is not to be cheap but to be responsible with the company's resources.

Meals are a common area of confusion. Generally, meals are 50% deductible, meaning you can only deduct half of the cost. However, there are some exceptions to this rule. For example, meals provided to employees for the convenience of the employer on the employer's premises may be fully deductible. Also, meals included in the price of a business conference or seminar may be fully deductible. Keep in mind that the "lavish or extravagant" rule also applies to meals. Just because you can deduct 50% of a meal doesn't mean you can spend exorbitant amounts of money. The meal must be reasonable under the circumstances. As you can see, even something seemingly straightforward as a business meal can be fraught with complexities. It is critical to ensure everything is properly documented.

Finally, let's discuss the importance of a robust T&E policy. A well-defined policy serves as a guide for employees, outlining what expenses are reimbursable, what documentation is required, and the process for submitting expense reports. The policy should be clear, concise, and easily accessible to all employees. It should also be regularly reviewed and updated to reflect changes in tax law or company practices. A strong T&E policy not only helps ensure compliance with IRS regulations but also promotes transparency and accountability within the organization. It sends a message to employees that the company takes T&E expenses seriously and is committed to following the rules. For shareholders, a robust policy signals good governance and responsible financial management. It demonstrates that the company is not only focused on generating profits but also on managing its expenses effectively and ethically. The company's tax practices should be transparent.

5.5 Home Office Deduction

The home office deduction can be a significant tax saver for shareholders of closely held companies who operate their businesses from their homes. It allows taxpayers to deduct expenses related to the portion of their home that is used exclusively and regularly for business. However, navigating the rules surrounding this deduction requires careful attention to detail, to avoid IRS scrutiny.

First and foremost, to qualify for the home office deduction, the space in your home must be used exclusively and regularly for business purposes. This means the area must be used solely for your business; a corner of your living room that doubles as your workspace likely wouldn't qualify. "Regularly" implies consistent and ongoing use for your business activities. Occasional or incidental business use does not meet this requirement. Remember, commingling personal and business use within the same space can disqualify the deduction. Think of it this way: if you're watching television in your "office" after business hours, it's no longer exclusively used for business.

Next, the area you're claiming for the home office deduction must be either your principal place of business, a place where you meet or deal with clients or customers in the normal course of your business, or a separate structure not attached to your home that you use in connection with your business. For most shareholders running small businesses, the "principal place of business" test is the most relevant. This generally means it's where you conduct the majority of your administrative or management activities, even if you conduct other business activities elsewhere. If you conduct a significant amount of your business outside your home, determining if your home office is the principal place can be complicated and needs deeper consideration to ensure its validity.

Calculating the deduction involves determining the percentage of your home used for business. There are two main methods for this: the simplified option and the regular method. The simplified option allows you to multiply a prescribed amount (currently $5 per square foot, up to a maximum of 300 square feet) by the square footage of your home office. This method is straightforward but often results in a smaller deduction compared to the regular method. The regular method involves calculating the actual expenses allocable to the home office. This requires determining the percentage of your home used for business, typically by dividing the square footage of your office by the total square footage of your home. This percentage is then applied to your total home expenses, such as mortgage interest (or rent), utilities, insurance, and depreciation.

Record-keeping is critical when claiming the home office deduction. Keep detailed records of all home-related expenses, including mortgage statements, rent receipts, utility bills, and insurance policies. It's also a good idea to document the size of your home and the square footage of your home office. Photographs of your home office can also be helpful in substantiating your claim. Poor documentation is a common reason why home office deductions are challenged during audits. Maintain a clear and organized system for tracking these expenses, making it easier to substantiate your claim if necessary. I advise keeping a separate folder (physical or digital) specifically for these records.

Depreciation is a key component of the home office deduction if you own your home. You can deduct depreciation on the portion of your home used for business. This requires calculating the depreciable basis of your home (generally the original cost plus improvements) and applying the business-use percentage. Depreciation can be complex, and it's often advisable to consult with a tax professional to ensure accurate calculations and compliance with IRS guidelines. Don't forget that claiming depreciation can affect the basis of your home when you eventually sell it, potentially leading to a larger capital gain.

Importantly, the home office deduction is limited to the gross income derived from your business. This means you can't use the deduction to create a loss. If your home office expenses exceed your business income, the excess expenses can be carried forward to future years, subject to the same limitation. This ensures that the deduction is directly tied to your business's profitability. This also means that if your business is struggling, the home office deduction may not provide immediate tax relief.

Moreover, if you are an employee, your ability to take the home office deduction is severely restricted. Due to changes made by the Tax Cuts and Jobs Act of 2017, employees can no longer deduct home office expenses. This restriction primarily affects shareholders who are also employees of their corporations. The deduction is generally only available to self-employed individuals, independent contractors, and those operating businesses as sole proprietorships, partnerships, or LLCs taxed as such.

As a closely held business owner, understanding the implications of the home office deduction is vital. It can provide significant tax savings, but requires meticulous record-keeping and a thorough understanding of the rules. Weigh the benefits against the potential for increased scrutiny from the IRS and determine if the deduction aligns with your business operations. A consultation with a tax professional can provide personalized guidance and ensure compliance with all applicable tax laws.

6 Chapter 6: Liabilities and Equity Analysis

Let's dive into liabilities and equity, components that paint a vivid picture of a company's financial standing and its future trajectory. Understanding these elements is crucial for shareholders because they reflect the company's obligations and ownership structure, influencing everything from risk assessment to dividend prospects.

First, consider liabilities. These are the debts a company owes to others – think loans, accounts payable, and deferred revenue. Their composition and management significantly impact a company's tax strategy. For example, interest paid on debt is often tax-deductible, incentivizing companies to use debt financing strategically. The classification of liabilities matters too: current liabilities (due within one year) signal immediate obligations, while long-term liabilities (due beyond one year) represent sustained financial commitments. Reviewing the schedule of liabilities provided in the financial statement notes will give the shareholders a better view of the financial health of the corporation and how the debt affects the business. Analyzing these schedules enables insights into the company's cash flow obligations and interest expenses, which directly affect taxable income. Now, how does a shareholder interpret this information? A high level of short-term debt relative to current assets might indicate liquidity issues, potentially impacting the company's ability to meet its obligations and invest in growth. Conversely, a manageable debt load, especially with favorable interest rates, can free up capital for expansion and shareholder returns.

Now, let's pivot to shareholder equity. This is the residual interest in the assets of the company after deducting liabilities; in simpler terms, it's what would be left for shareholders if all assets were sold and all debts were paid. The most basic elements of the shareholders' equity are the common stock, preferred stock and the treasury stock. Within this framework, retained earnings holds particular significance. It's the accumulated net income of the company that has not been distributed to shareholders as dividends. A growing retained earnings balance generally indicates a profitable and financially healthy company, signaling that the company is generating profits and reinvesting them for future growth. However, it's crucial to dig deeper. A massive build-up of retained earnings without a corresponding increase in investment or dividend payouts might suggest inefficient capital allocation or potential tax implications for the company and its shareholders. A corporation that retains its earning does not pay taxes for those earnings but the shareholders do not see any money back.

Delving deeper into retained earnings, consider the impact of dividends. Dividends are distributions of a company's profits to its shareholders, and they have direct tax implications. From the company's perspective, dividends are not tax-deductible, unlike interest payments on debt. From the shareholder's perspective, dividends are generally taxable as income, although the specific tax rate depends on the type of dividend (qualified vs. non-qualified) and the shareholder's individual tax bracket. A company's dividend policy – whether it chooses to pay regular dividends, increase dividends over time, or reinvest profits – can significantly impact shareholder returns and tax liabilities. It's not just about the amount of the dividend; it's about the signaling effect. A consistent dividend payout can signal stability and confidence in the company's future prospects, attracting long-term investors. However, a sudden increase or decrease in dividends can also raise questions and potentially impact the stock price. When shareholders get dividends they must pay the taxes for those dividends.

Equity also encompasses items like Additional Paid-In Capital (APIC), which represents the amount investors paid for stock in excess of its par value, and treasury stock, which is the company's own stock that it has repurchased from the market. Treasury stock can be used for various purposes, such as employee stock options or to increase earnings per share, and its tax implications depend on how it's utilized. APIC has no tax implications.

Another crucial element to consider is the impact of stock-based compensation on both the company's financial statements and the shareholder's tax situation. Stock options and restricted stock units (RSUs) are often used to incentivize employees and align their interests with those of the shareholders. While the company gets a tax deduction when employees exercise their stock options or RSUs vest, the employees are then subject to income tax on the difference between the market price of the stock and the exercise price (for options) or the fair market value (for RSUs). From a shareholder's perspective, stock-based compensation can dilute ownership and potentially reduce earnings per share. A clear understanding of a company's stock-based compensation plans is therefore essential for assessing its long-term financial health and potential tax implications for both the company and its employees. For the employees the advantage is the fact that they are given the possibility to buy a share at a lower price than the market price.

In summary, understanding liabilities and equity requires a multifaceted approach. It's not just about the numbers on the balance sheet; it's about understanding the story behind those numbers and their impact on a company's financial health, tax position, and shareholder value. By carefully analyzing debt obligations, shareholder equity components, and dividend policies, shareholders can gain valuable insights into a company's long-term prospects and make more informed investment decisions. Furthermore, understanding the tax implications of different financial strategies can help shareholders optimize their investment returns and navigate the complexities of the financial landscape. By paying close attention to these key elements, shareholders can unlock a deeper understanding of a company's financial narrative and make more informed decisions.

6.1 Understanding Debt Obligations

Let's delve into the realm of debt obligations. Understanding these liabilities is paramount for shareholders seeking a clear picture of a company's financial health and tax position. After all, debt isn't just a number on a balance sheet; it's a commitment with significant implications for future cash flows, profitability, and ultimately, shareholder value.

Debt obligations represent a company's commitments to repay borrowed funds. These commitments can take many forms, from short-term lines of credit to long-term bonds issued to finance significant capital projects. The key is to distinguish between different types of debt, as each carries its own set of risks and tax implications. For example, a revolving credit facility, often used for working capital needs, might have variable interest rates that fluctuate with market conditions. This introduces interest rate risk, where unexpected rate hikes can squeeze profits. On the other hand, a fixed-rate term loan provides more predictable interest expenses, but might come with restrictive covenants that limit the company's operational flexibility, such as restrictions on dividend payouts or further borrowing.

Interest expense, a direct consequence of debt, is generally tax-deductible. This reduces a company's taxable income, effectively lowering its tax burden. However, the deductibility of interest is not unlimited. Tax laws often place restrictions on the amount of interest that can be deducted, particularly in cases of excessive leverage or related-party lending. Analyzing a company's debt structure and interest expense in relation to its earnings before interest, taxes, depreciation, and amortization (EBITDA) provides insights into its ability to service its debt obligations and the potential impact of these limitations on its tax liabilities. Furthermore, understanding the specific terms of the debt agreements, including any covenants, is crucial. These covenants can significantly affect a company's strategic options and may even trigger default if violated.

Beyond the simple deduction of interest expense, debt can also create other tax implications. For instance, the issuance of debt at a discount (original issue discount or OID) requires the issuer to amortize that discount over the life of the debt, creating a non-cash expense that affects taxable income. Similarly, the repurchase of debt at a price different from its face value can result in a taxable gain or loss for the company. These nuances highlight the importance of carefully examining the footnotes to the financial statements, where detailed information about debt obligations and their tax treatment is typically disclosed. Shareholders should scrutinize these disclosures to fully understand the tax implications of the company's debt management strategies.

It is not uncommon for companies to engage in debt restructuring, either voluntarily or due to financial distress. These restructurings can have significant tax consequences. For example, if a company exchanges old debt for new debt with different terms, or if it cancels a portion of its debt, it may realize cancellation of debt (COD) income. COD income is generally taxable, although there are exceptions for companies in bankruptcy or those that are considered insolvent. Understanding the tax rules surrounding debt restructuring is essential for assessing the true financial impact of such transactions.

Convertible debt adds another layer of complexity. This type of debt can be converted into equity shares, offering the holder the potential for capital appreciation if the company's stock price increases. From a tax perspective, the conversion of debt into equity generally does not result in an immediate taxable event for the company. However, the accounting treatment of convertible debt can affect earnings per share calculations and other financial metrics, which in turn can influence shareholder perceptions.

Leases, while technically not debt, can function as a form of financing and should be considered in any analysis of a company's debt obligations. Under accounting standards, many leases are now recognized on the balance sheet as liabilities, similar to debt. This "capitalization" of leases increases a company's reported debt levels and can affect its financial ratios. The tax treatment of leases can also be complex, with different rules applying to operating leases and capital leases. Shareholders should carefully analyze a company's lease obligations and their impact on both its financial statements and its tax liabilities.

Analyzing debt requires careful attention to the details. Look at the maturity dates of the debt. A company with a large amount of debt maturing in the near future may face refinancing challenges, especially in a rising interest rate environment. The credit ratings assigned to a company's debt also provide valuable information about its creditworthiness and the likelihood of default. A lower credit rating typically indicates a higher risk of default and can lead to higher borrowing costs. Furthermore, it's important to compare a company's debt levels to those of its peers in the same industry. This can help identify whether a company is overleveraged or conservatively financed.

In conclusion, understanding a company's debt obligations is crucial for assessing its financial health and potential tax liabilities. By carefully examining the different types of debt, the terms of the debt agreements, and the related tax implications, shareholders can gain a deeper understanding of the company's financial position and make more informed investment decisions. Always read the footnotes, analyze the ratios, and compare the company to its peers. This is your responsibility as a shareholder seeking clarity.

6.2 Shareholder Equity Components

Delving into shareholder equity, we find it's far more than just a number on a balance sheet. It represents the owners' stake in the company, what would be left over for them if all assets were sold and all liabilities were paid off. It's a key indicator of a company's financial health and its ability to grow and return value to its shareholders. But shareholder equity is not a single, monolithic figure; it's composed of several distinct components, each with its own significance and tax implications.

The first, and perhaps most straightforward, component is common stock. This represents the basic ownership units of the corporation. The par value of common stock, often a nominal amount, is recorded separately from any additional paid-in capital. When shares are issued at a price exceeding their par value, the excess amount is recorded as additional paid-in capital. This distinction is important from an accounting perspective, though it often has limited direct tax implications for the shareholder. From a shareholder's perspective, understanding the number of authorized, issued, and outstanding shares is vital. Authorized shares are the total number a company is legally allowed to issue. Issued shares are those the company has actually sold. Outstanding shares are those held by investors (issued shares minus any shares repurchased by the company – treasury stock). These numbers can impact earnings per share calculations and voting power.

Next, we consider preferred stock. Unlike common stock, preferred

stock typically grants its holders certain preferences over common stockholders, such as priority in dividend payments or asset distribution during liquidation. These preferences come at a cost, as preferred stock often lacks the voting rights associated with common stock. The tax implications of preferred stock can be complex, particularly concerning dividend taxation. Dividends paid on preferred stock are generally treated as dividend income for the recipient, subject to applicable tax rates. For the issuing corporation, dividends paid are not deductible expenses, unlike interest payments on debt.
Retained earnings constitute another critical piece of the shareholder equity puzzle. This represents the accumulated profits of the company that have not been distributed to shareholders as dividends. Retained earnings are a testament to a company's profitability and its ability to reinvest earnings back into the business. The larger the retained earnings balance, the more financially stable the company generally appears. Tax-wise, retained earnings themselves aren't directly taxed. However, the activities that generate retained earnings – profits – are subject to corporate income tax. Furthermore, the decisions regarding the distribution of retained earnings, specifically through dividends, have significant tax consequences for shareholders, as dividends are typically taxable income. The accumulation of excessive retained earnings may also attract scrutiny from tax authorities, particularly if it appears the company is avoiding shareholder taxes by hoarding profits.

Treasury stock, another important aspect, represents shares of the company's own stock that have been repurchased from the market. These shares are no longer considered outstanding and are held by the company. Treasury stock reduces shareholder equity because it effectively represents a distribution of corporate assets back to shareholders. There are various reasons why a company might repurchase its own shares, including boosting earnings per share, signaling confidence in the company's future, or having shares available for em-

ployee stock options or acquisitions. Tax implications related to treasury stock are generally associated with the initial repurchase (which may be treated as a dividend in certain circumstances) and the subsequent reissuance of the shares. When treasury stock is reissued, any difference between the repurchase price and the reissuance price is typically recorded as an adjustment to additional paid-in capital.
Accumulated other comprehensive income (AOCI) is a less frequently discussed, yet equally significant, component of shareholder equity. This includes items that are not reported on the income statement, such as unrealized gains and losses on available-for-sale securities, foreign currency translation adjustments, and certain pension-related adjustments. These items are considered "comprehensive income" because they represent changes in equity from non-owner sources. The tax implications of AOCI are varied and depend on the specific item. For example, unrealized gains on securities are not taxed until the securities are actually sold. Foreign currency translation adjustments generally do not have immediate tax consequences. Understanding AOCI is crucial for a complete picture of a company's financial performance and its potential future tax liabilities.

Analyzing these shareholder equity components requires a nuanced approach, as each piece contributes to the overall financial health and tax position of the company. Investors and analysts must consider the relative proportions of each component, the trends over time, and the potential tax implications to gain a thorough understanding of the company's value and future prospects. Reviewing historical records of changes in shareholder equity can provide valuable insights into management's decisions regarding capital structure, dividend policy, and strategic investments.

6.3 Retained Earnings Analysis

Retained earnings represent the cumulative net income of a company after accounting for dividends paid to shareholders. Analyzing this account is critical for shareholders because it provides insights into a company's profitability, dividend policy, and overall financial health. A healthy and growing retained earnings balance often indicates a company that is generating profits and reinvesting them back into the business, leading to potential future growth and increased shareholder value. However, simply looking at the number isn't enough; you need to delve deeper to understand the story it tells.

Begin by examining the trend of retained earnings over several periods, typically three to five years. A consistent upward trend suggests strong profitability and effective management of resources. A fluctuating pattern might indicate inconsistent performance or strategic changes that warrant further investigation. A declining balance, especially over a prolonged period, can be a red flag, suggesting losses, excessive dividend payouts, or other financial difficulties. Compare the company's retained earnings growth rate to its industry peers. If the company is lagging behind, it might indicate competitive disadvantages or operational inefficiencies. Don't just look at the absolute numbers; consider them in relation to the company's size and industry. A small increase in retained earnings for a large company might be insignificant, while the same increase for a smaller company could be substantial. Remember, a trend is just a trend until it bends. Look for events or circumstances that may explain sudden changes in the retained earnings balance.

Furthermore, it's essential to understand how retained earnings are impacted by dividend policy. A company that pays out a large portion of its earnings as dividends will naturally have lower retained earnings. While dividends are attractive to shareholders seeking immediate income, a high dividend payout ratio might limit the company's ability to reinvest in growth opportunities. Analyze the company's dividend payout ratio (dividends paid divided by net income) over time. A stable or increasing payout ratio might indicate a mature company with limited growth prospects, while a low or decreasing ratio suggests that the company is prioritizing reinvestment. Consider the industry context; some industries, like utilities, typically have higher dividend payout ratios than others, like technology. It's crucial to understand if the dividend policy is aligned with the company's overall strategic goals. Is the company prioritizing short-term shareholder returns over long-term growth? Are the dividends sustainable given the company's financial performance? A dividend cut can be a major blow to shareholder confidence, so it's important to assess the likelihood of such an event.

Beyond dividends, retained earnings can be affected by various accounting adjustments and transactions. For instance, prior period adjustments, which correct errors in previously issued financial statements, can significantly impact retained earnings. These adjustments should be carefully scrutinized to understand the nature of the error and its potential impact on past financial performance. Also, stock-based compensation expense, while not a cash outflow, reduces net income and, consequently, retained earnings. Keep an eye out for significant changes in stock-based compensation plans, as they can affect reported profitability. Understanding the notes to the financial statements is crucial, as they often provide detailed explanations of these adjustments and transactions. Pay close attention to any restatements of prior period financial statements, as these can indicate serious accounting issues. Also, be aware of changes in accounting standards, as they can affect the way retained earnings are calculated and reported. Remember that accounting is not an exact science, and there is room for interpretation and judgment. It is important to assess whether the company's accounting policies are conservative or aggressive, as this can affect the reliability of the retained earnings

balance.
Looking at the relationship between retained earnings and other financial metrics is also vital. For example, comparing retained earnings to total equity can provide insights into the proportion of equity that is derived from accumulated profits versus other sources, such as contributed capital. A high ratio of retained earnings to total equity suggests a company that has been consistently profitable and has relied less on external funding. Also, consider the relationship between retained earnings and the company's growth rate. A company that is growing rapidly might need to reinvest a significant portion of its earnings, resulting in lower retained earnings. It's important to assess whether the company's growth is sustainable given its current level of profitability and retained earnings. A company that is relying heavily on debt financing to fund its growth might be at risk if it experiences a downturn in its business. Understanding these interrelationships provides a more holistic view of the company's financial health and its ability to generate future returns for shareholders. Compare it to other equity accounts like common stock and additional paid-in capital.
Finally, always remember that retained earnings is just one piece of the puzzle. It's essential to consider it in conjunction with other financial metrics, industry trends, and the overall economic environment. Don't rely solely on retained earnings to make investment decisions. Perform a thorough analysis of the company's financial statements and business prospects. Consider seeking advice from a qualified financial advisor if you have any questions or concerns. The financial markets are complex and ever-changing, and it's important to stay informed and make informed investment decisions. By taking a comprehensive approach to analyzing retained earnings, you can gain valuable insights into a company's financial health and its potential to create long-term shareholder value.

7 Chapter 7: Advanced Tax Planning Strategies

Now, let's dive into the realm of advanced tax planning. This is where savvy financial management truly shines, transforming potential tax burdens into opportunities for growth and reinvestment. It goes far beyond simple expense tracking and delves into strategic maneuvers, utilizing the full arsenal of tax laws and incentives to optimize a company's financial position. It's about not just avoiding overpayment, but actively shaping the company's operations to achieve the most advantageous tax outcomes.

Consider, for instance, the strategic use of tax credits. These aren't just "nice to haves"; they can be game-changers, significantly reducing a company's tax liability dollar for dollar. Research and Development (R&D) tax credits are a prime example. Many companies, particularly in technology, manufacturing, and even service industries, overlook the potential for claiming R&D credits. The definition of "research and development" for tax purposes is often broader than many initially assume, encompassing activities related to developing new products, processes, or even improving existing ones. Thorough documentation is crucial here. You need detailed records of the projects, the costs involved, and the specific innovations achieved. This meticulous approach not only supports the credit claim but also demonstrates a proactive and compliant tax strategy. Furthermore, explore energy efficiency credits, often available for companies investing in renewable energy sources or energy-saving equipment. These credits not only benefit the environment but also contribute to a company's bottom line, showcasing a commitment to sustainability while simultaneously reducing tax obligations. However, it is important to remember that tax credits are subject to change depending on legislation, it is important to stay up to date on the current legislation.

Another powerful tool in advanced tax planning is strategic timing. Deferring income and accelerating deductions can significantly impact a company's cash flow and overall tax liability. For example, consider the timing of large sales or projects. If a company anticipates a significant increase in its tax rate in the coming year, it might be advantageous to accelerate income recognition into the current year, even if it means offering slight discounts or incentives to customers. Conversely, accelerating deductions can be beneficial if a company anticipates lower tax rates in the future. This can be achieved by prepaying certain expenses, such as insurance premiums or rent, or by making strategic investments in depreciable assets that qualify for accelerated depreciation. The key is to carefully analyze the company's projected income, expenses, and tax rates, then aligning financial activities to maximize tax efficiency over the long term. However, there should be a clear plan and a valid purpose.

Furthermore, consider the strategic use of different business entities. The choice of business structure – whether it's a C corporation, S corporation, partnership, or LLC – can have significant tax implications. C corporations, for example, are subject to double taxation, while S corporations and partnerships offer pass-through taxation. However, C corporations also offer the advantage of retaining earnings for future growth without immediate taxation at the individual level. LLCs provide flexibility in terms of management structure and liability protection, while partnerships allow for easy allocation of income and losses among partners. The best choice depends on the specific circumstances of the business, including its size, ownership structure, growth plans, and tolerance for risk. Consulting with a tax professional is essential to determine the optimal business structure and to navigate the complexities of state and local tax laws.

Moreover, international tax planning presents both opportunities and challenges for multinational corporations. Transfer pricing, which involves the pricing of goods, services, and intellectual property transferred between related entities in different countries, is a critical area of focus. Tax authorities closely scrutinize transfer pricing arrangements to ensure that they are arm's length and that companies are not shifting profits to lower-tax jurisdictions. Compliance with transfer pricing regulations requires thorough documentation, economic analysis, and a deep understanding of the tax laws in each country where the company operates. However, international tax planning also offers opportunities to optimize a company's global tax burden through strategic structuring, treaty utilization, and effective management of foreign tax credits.

Tax planning is not a one-size-fits-all approach. What works for one company may not work for another. It requires a deep understanding of the company's specific circumstances, its industry, and the ever-changing tax landscape. That's why it's so crucial to build a strong relationship with a qualified tax advisor who can provide personalized guidance and help the company navigate the complexities of tax law. Moreover, stay updated, the tax landscape is always changing.

7.1 Tax Credits and Incentives

Tax credits and incentives, often overlooked in the labyrinthine world of corporate taxation, represent a potent tool for businesses to reduce their tax liabilities and enhance profitability. As a shareholder, understanding these mechanisms is crucial, providing insights into a company's strategic tax planning and its commitment to maximizing shareholder value. These provisions are not merely loopholes; they are deliberate policy instruments enacted by governments to encourage specific economic activities or social behaviors.

The landscape of tax credits is vast and varied, shaped by federal, state, and local jurisdictions, each with its own set of objectives. At the federal level, the Research and Development (R&D) Tax Credit stands out as a significant opportunity for companies investing in innovation. This credit incentivizes businesses to engage in qualified research activities, reducing the after-tax cost of developing new products, processes, or software. To qualify, activities must meet specific criteria, including technological in nature, intended to discover new information, and aimed at developing a new or improved business component. The calculation can be complex, involving qualified research expenses (QREs) such as wages, supplies, and contract research. Companies often engage specialized consultants to navigate the intricacies of documenting and substantiating their R&D activities to maximize the credit.

Another noteworthy federal incentive is the Work Opportunity Tax Credit (WOTC), designed to encourage employers to hire individuals from targeted groups, such as veterans, ex-felons, or those receiving public assistance. By hiring eligible individuals, companies can claim a credit based on a percentage of the employee's first-year wages. The WOTC not only reduces a company's tax burden but also promotes social responsibility and workforce diversity. Eligibility requirements can be strict, necessitating careful screening and documentation of new hires. State-level incentives are frequently tailored to promote local economic development, targeting specific industries or geographic areas. Many states offer tax credits for job creation, investment in renewable energy, or revitalization of distressed communities. These incentives can be particularly attractive to businesses considering expansion or relocation, offering substantial tax savings and other benefits. For example, a company establishing a manufacturing facility in an economically disadvantaged zone might qualify for tax credits, property tax abatements, and workforce training grants.

Renewable energy tax credits are gaining increasing prominence as governments worldwide strive to transition to cleaner energy sources. The federal government offers tax credits for investments in solar, wind, and other renewable energy projects. These credits can significantly reduce the cost of implementing renewable energy systems, making them more economically viable for businesses. Many states also offer their own renewable energy incentives, further enhancing the financial attractiveness of these investments. Beyond these broad categories, tax credits and incentives are available for a wide range of activities, including historic preservation, energy efficiency improvements, and charitable contributions. Understanding the specific requirements and eligibility criteria for each incentive is crucial for businesses seeking to maximize their tax benefits.

Navigating the landscape of tax credits and incentives requires a proactive and strategic approach. Companies must carefully assess their operations and investment plans to identify potential opportunities for claiming these benefits. Thorough documentation is essential to support credit claims, including detailed records of expenses, activities, and eligibility criteria. Engaging tax professionals with expertise in this area can be invaluable in identifying and maximizing available incentives. These experts can provide guidance on eligibility requirements, documentation procedures, and potential pitfalls. It's important to consider the timing of investments and activities to align with credit eligibility periods. Some incentives may have expiration dates or annual limitations, requiring careful planning to ensure maximum benefit.

Moreover, companies should be aware of the potential for changes in tax laws and regulations. Tax codes are subject to frequent updates and revisions, which can impact the availability and value of tax credits and incentives. Staying informed about these changes is crucial for effective tax planning. As a shareholder, staying informed about a company's tax strategies and its utilization of tax credits and incentives can provide valuable insights into its financial performance and its commitment to responsible corporate citizenship. Ask informed questions during shareholder meetings, review the company's financial statements, and consider the long-term implications of its tax planning decisions. By understanding these incentives, you can better assess the company's financial health and its ability to deliver sustainable value. Remember that tax credits are not simply a way to avoid paying taxes; they are a strategic tool that can drive innovation, create jobs, and promote sustainable development. A company that effectively utilizes these incentives is likely to be a more competitive and successful enterprise.

7.2 Minimizing Tax Liabilities

Tax planning isn't just about crunching numbers; it's about understanding the entire financial landscape of a company and strategically positioning assets and operations to minimize tax obligations while remaining fully compliant. For shareholders, grasping these strategies is paramount to evaluating the long-term profitability and sustainability of their investments. The goal is not to evade taxes – that's illegal and unethical – but to legally reduce the tax burden through proactive planning and careful consideration of available options.

A crucial first step is understanding the different types of tax credits and incentives available to businesses. These can range from research and development (R&D) tax credits, which reward companies for investing in innovation, to energy efficiency tax credits, designed to encourage environmentally friendly practices. Many jurisdictions also offer specific incentives for businesses operating in designated enterprise zones or those hiring individuals from disadvantaged backgrounds. Thorough due diligence is required to identify applicable credits and ensure eligibility. This often involves consulting with tax professionals who specialize in these areas, as the requirements and application processes can be complex and vary significantly by jurisdiction. The impact of these credits can be substantial, directly reducing a company's tax bill and improving its bottom line. Keep in mind that these incentives aren't static. They evolve with changing government policies and priorities. Stay updated on the latest legislative changes to capitalize on new opportunities and avoid missing out on expiring credits.

Beyond tax credits, carefully structuring business operations can yield significant tax savings. For instance, choosing the optimal legal structure for a business – whether it's a C corporation, S corporation, partnership, or limited liability company (LLC) – has significant tax implications. Each structure has different rules regarding taxation of profits, losses, and distributions to owners. Consulting with a tax advisor to determine the most advantageous structure based on a company's specific circumstances and long-term goals is essential. Moreover, strategic asset allocation can also play a role in minimizing taxes. Depreciating assets, such as equipment and buildings, over their useful lives allows businesses to deduct a portion of their cost each year, reducing taxable income. Accelerating depreciation using methods like the Modified Accelerated Cost Recovery System (MACRS) can provide even larger deductions in the early years of an asset's life, further reducing tax liabilities. Furthermore, businesses can utilize strategies like like-kind exchanges (under Section 1031 of the Internal Revenue Code in the US) to defer capital gains taxes when selling and reinvesting in similar assets. This allows businesses to upgrade their assets without immediately incurring a tax liability. Another often overlooked area is international tax planning. For multinational corporations, managing tax obligations across different countries can be a complex but potentially rewarding endeavor. Strategies like transfer pricing – setting prices for goods and services exchanged between related entities in different countries – can significantly impact a company's overall tax burden. However, transfer pricing is subject to strict regulations and scrutiny by tax authorities, so it's crucial to ensure that these prices are arm's length, meaning they reflect the prices that would be charged between unrelated parties in a similar transaction. Establishing holding companies in jurisdictions with favorable tax laws can also be a legitimate way to minimize taxes on international profits. Careful planning and compliance with international tax treaties are essential to avoid potential penalties and disputes with tax authorities. Remember, engaging with international tax experts is crucial here, since regulations change often and each jurisdiction is different.

Effective tax planning is not a one-time event but an ongoing process that requires continuous monitoring and adaptation. Tax laws are constantly evolving, and businesses must stay informed of these changes to ensure compliance and identify new opportunities for tax savings. Regular tax reviews, conducted by qualified tax professionals, can help identify potential issues and ensure that a company is taking advantage of all available tax benefits. Furthermore, maintaining accurate and complete financial records is crucial for supporting tax positions and avoiding penalties in the event of an audit. Proper documentation is the cornerstone of any successful tax planning strategy. Finally, understand that tax planning should be integrated with overall business strategy. Tax considerations should be factored into major business decisions, such as mergers and acquisitions, expansions, and restructurings. By taking a proactive and holistic approach to tax planning, companies can minimize their tax liabilities, improve their financial performance, and enhance shareholder value. It requires diligence, expertise, and a commitment to ethical and compliant tax practices.

www.ingramcontent.com/pod-product-compliance
Ingram Content Group UK Ltd.
Pitfield, Milton Keynes, MK11 3LW, UK
UKHW020157290926
15471UKWH00005B/928

9 798349 521539